SACRED SEX AND MAGICK

In *Sacred Sex and Magick*, the folks at the Web PATH Center have provided a concise, real-world look at a subject which is for once not treated either as titillation or steeped in arcane language. In this book, the authors have stripped away a number of common biases and misconceptions; everyone regardless of personal preferences can find a natural fit within these exercises and meditations; likewise the personal experiences shared will resonate with a wide range of readers. While the focus is obviously on sexual magick, much of what's covered here is readily applied to non-sexual practices as well.

Kurt Hohmann is the coordinator for the Central New York Pagan Pride Project, Assistant Pagan Chaplain at Syracuse University, New York State Steward for the Troth, and founding member of two local pagan groups in and around Syracuse New York.

Pagan Portals
Sacred Sex and Magick

Pagan Portals
Sacred Sex
and Magick

Web PATH Center

Winchester, UK
Washington, USA

First published by Moon Books, 2015
Moon Books is an imprint of John Hunt Publishing Ltd., Laurel House, Station Approach,
Alresford, Hants, SO24 9JH, UK
office1@jhpbooks.net
www.johnhuntpublishing.com
www.moon-books.net

For distributor details and how to order please visit the 'Ordering' section on our website.

Text copyright: Web PATH Center 2014

ISBN: 978 1 78279 554 4

A CIP catalogue record for this book is available from the British Library.

Design: Stuart Davies
www.stuartdaviesart.com

Printed and bound by CPI Group (UK) Ltd, Croydon, CR0 4YY, UK

We operate a distinctive and ethical publishing philosophy in all
areas of our business, from our global network of authors to
production and worldwide distribution.

CONTENTS

Preface   1

Introduction   10

Chapter 1. Contemporary Paganism and Sex Magick:
            What is Going on Now?   19

Chapter 2. Contemporary Paganism: How is Sacred Sex
            Used in Ritual?   36

Chapter 3. Recognizing the Chakras in Sex Magick   57

Chapter 4. Spirit Lovers   64

Chapter 5. Our Best Advice   73

Who we are and what process did we used to write the book?

The Web PATH Center is a pagan church located in Lyons, New York. We have been around since 1993, leading rituals, teaching classes, celebrating the full moon and the sabbats around the wheel of the year. We are an open teaching circle, as any church in the USA is required to be under federal tax law. Members of the public are welcome, and sometimes walk in. We sit in ritual space within a cast circle, teaching as we go. No one has ever disrupted a service. Our church is a store front in a village. We intend to manifest a place in the country, but we have not been able to do that yet.

There are about 18 people behind the words you are reading. Here is what they say about themselves.

Anemone Webweaver is the scribe. She and her partner Merlin are two of the founding members of the Web PATH Center. They are our elders, retired and more magickal than ever. You may know Anemone by her mundane name Dorothy L. Abrams, author of *Identity and the Quartered Circle*. She has been a feminist and woman's advocate, civil rights investigator and high school teacher.

Merlin was born in the UK and has lived his adult live in the USA. Merlin and Anemone hosted the Web PATH Center in their home until 2007 when they began re-discovering Great Britain. They developed most of the Wicca training courses 1-4 taught at the Web. Merlin serves as the man in black for our rituals. Merlin also counts himself a feminist, one who works with balanced polarity and insists on working in open groups that embrace men, women and transgendered people. He has been a civil rights investigator, health program administrator, army medic, auto mechanic, heavy equipment operator and early childhood educator.

Galadriel has been a practicing Wiccan witch for 15 years. She has served on the Web Council of Trustees as chair and treasurer and completed all four levels of Wicca training. She is currently studying with the Sisterhood of Avalon. Galadriel is a pagan priestess, shamanic worker, teacher and Reiki Master. She studied horticulture in college and has an excellent green thumb. She and her family host the Web's SummerFest event, which entails a tremendous commitment. She and her teenage daughter lead ritual together for the Web several times a year.

Sappirewolf joined the Web in 2004. She has been Council chair for two years and served on our Council for six years. She has raised two young adult offspring, one who is decidedly pagan and the other who is non-denominational. She is a Web teacher, healer and Reiki Master who has completed all four levels of Web Wicca training. She has been one of the lead ritualists and priestesses for our sabbats and esbats.

Silver Lightning followed his wife Sappirewolf to the Web and took the first two levels of Wicca classes. He is fire keeper and man in black for the Web. He is most at home walking in the woods with Cernuous and the forest spirits, but he does help teach Wicca I classes, particular in sessions about the earth spirits and Gods.

Satira is an eclectic who is more than the sum total of her parts. She has completed all four levels of Web training. She is a channeler from birth who attempts to translate deep esoteric knowledge into this dimension. She is currently working with elemental spirits across the dimensions and other planets to assist in rebalancing all of us as we proceed through the planetary shifts and realignments of our time.

Moonhawk is presently an EMT (Emergency Medical Tech) as paid staff on ambulance service. He recently completed Wicca I and intends to keep on learning. He focuses on healing and helping others, anticipating classes in Reiki, runes and Wicca II, which carries the initiation of the healer. As new neighbors of Merlin and Anemone, he is loving country living for himself, his children, his bride Ivy Moon and her children. He has worked as a stock clerk, cook, factory worker, truck driver, and served in the U.S. Navy before finding his career as an EMT.

Ivy Moon is a solitary witch celebrating the wheel of the year in Central NY. She came across the Web PATH around 2004. She completed two levels of Wiccan classes at the Web and looks forward to taking more with Moonhawk. Ivy Moon is a mother to his and her children. Professionally she is a caregiver for the mentally challenged. Her interests on the pagan path include simple household spell work using oils and herbs and meddling with candle making for spells. In healing work, she makes steam inhalants with oils and herbs. We count on her to send 'angels' out to those who request it.

Elly was formerly a teacher, artist, and woman of many concurrent nontraditional jobs. She is now retired to the country in the Finger Lakes, NY, as an eclectic farmer of unique and unusual trees and shrubs. She is a hedgewitch, mom to cows, chickens, cats and occasionally to her three grownup human children. She has served on the Web Council and is a key organizer for Web programs, finances and logistics. She is also magickal.

The Ditchwitch, aka Marie Snow Taber, is a woman who embraces many crafts. A trained herbalist, growing and wildcrafting herbs, food, and friends, she has been a professional belly dancer, and enjoys teaching this craft and sharing the joys of ecstasy. She, along with her husband Tall Corn, embody the truth of the joys of magick in their everyday lives, be it Green Magick, the magick of love and sex, and the magick of simply being alive! They enjoy sharing their lands with people who have reverence for earth. They have lived on Taber's Greenwood and Standing Stone Farm for more than 30 years. She has been a member of Web PATH Center since 2001 and completed all four levels of Web Wicca training, as well as other esoteric and tantric instruction from notable pagans around the world.

Pegqua has been a member of the Web PATH Center since 2001, participating as priestess, healer, and storyteller. She has served as assistant chair and Council chair. Pegqua has always felt the call of the Goddess and the Web PATH has assisted her to remember who she is. In the mundane world she is an LPN working with the elderly, and especially loves giving end-of-life care. She has completed three levels of Wicca training, and is our strongest trainer in pagan death and dying.

Stonefinder, Pegqua's husband has also been a member of the Web PATH Center since 2001. He is a healer and friend to the stone people, supplier of holey stones found in the Finger Lakes on the lake shore. As a spirit sensitive, he works with guides and entities who come to visit on this side of the veil, sometimes to the disquiet of people who think these places are haunted.

Stonelight Weaver, a member of the Web PATH Center since its inception, is a daughter, mother, grandmother, kitchenwitch and crone. In her youth she was mentored by teachers of spiritual light along many different paths. She has been a caterer and a social worker with her masters in not-for profit organization administration. She is currently a stone carver and a teacher of self-healing visualizations. She is very passionate about teaching the joy and benefits of preparing the earth's bounty in a respectful manner as her calling to the Goddess path. She has completed all four levels of Web Wiccan training.

Missy is a mother, grandmother and Reiki Master, who writes sometimes and does crafts when the mood strikes. She has spent her life taking care of others and wholeheartedly believes that is why she is here. Her mother used to call Missy her 'professional student' because she loves to learn new things. Music is a very important part of Missy's life. She has to listen and sing every day. She physically feels a loss when she has no music. She has completed all four levels of Web Wiccan training.

Willow Woman at age 75-plus looks back on a life of teaching and working with children and youth in various capacities and organizations. After her 40-year marriage ended, she found a committed and significant relationship with a man from the Hudson Valley. They married in 2013. She is a mother, grandmother and great-grandmother. She spent her younger and middle years as a Christian. Even then, though she didn't recognize it, pagan beliefs and practices were showing through naturally in her life. Several years ago she came into contact with the Web and knew she had found a place to learn what she needed to know in order for her spirit to grow and thrive.

Noel aka Ivy BlackBadger realized the need for the world's people to reconnect with Mother Earth and their Patrons; she began to reconnect herself at an age of 14. With her first few steps of her new journey, she broke her illusion of the 'world' she thought she knew by recreating a view lost to many people. Now 20 years of age, she continues to progress by helping others see behind the mainstream media to discover the things that naturally belong to us, but have been forgotten. She is an artist and single mom.

Shawn Marie is a lover, mother of two sons and, for the last seven years, a licensed massage therapist developing her skills in complementary healing arts. Her path has brought her to healing her sexual identity, reuniting passion with self-respect and with the meaning of true love. She chose this path not only for her spirit, but for her ancestral mothers. Learning to become vulnerable and confident in our sexual beings is a lifelong lesson, but one that has already brought a beautiful change in Shawn Marie's view of herself, her body and her expression of unity. For this she is eternally grateful.

Bekki Shining Bearheart is a shamanic teacher, licensed massage therapist and skilled healer. She is co-founder of the Church of Earth Healing and a member of the Web, dividing her time between Ohio and New York. She is available to teach public seminars described at http://church-of-earth-healing.org. She has presented shamanic instruction throughout the north east and mid-Atlantic states, Ohio and in the UK.

The Sacrificial Virgin, a 16-year-old who knows magick and ritual well enough to give us insights. No we did not really sacrifice her, but we do protect her identity. She is smart, creative and runs cross country track.

We began this book at a full moon ritual when the Goddess gave the scribe orders to write her story. The rest of us jumped in and asked to work as a group. The scribe was greatly relieved. We met at our 2013 SummerFest to begin working on the outline, asking questions and defining terms. Then we sent the scribe to comb through the computer files and put everything we had saved and taught for 20 years into that outline. She followed directions pretty well. Then she came back at us and gave us assignments. Some researched topics. Some channeled information. Others meditated. Several enjoyed practicing the concept of sacred sex with great vigor. They speak for themselves.

Gradually the book took shape, and here it is. *Sacred Sex and Magick.* We invite you to our journey, to dance the magick with us and celebrate the ecstasy.

Our Intention and Experience

Sexuality is magick and transformation. Isn't everything different after deeply satisfying sexual experiences? Orgasm raises power and releases it within the body, sending it outward. When a magickal intent has been formed between the lovers, then that power is directed toward their shared purpose. Balancing male and female energy in yourself with sexual orgasm, within yourself and a partner of opposite sex, or within different aspects of inner selves in partners of same sex brings a spiritual awareness to otherwise physical encounters. Simultaneous orgasm is not required to balance the energy. We are able to assist our partners in raising that energy up through the body when we don't come at the same time.

Sexual expression is a dynamic training ground for healing, openness, transformation, creativity and love. Ironically it is also so much fun, humankind is able to procreate and love without consciously engaging spirit at all, so most of us have missed the point and the experiences of spiritually ecstatic sex. Our ancestors may have done better in tribal practices. Or not. Maybe the priests and priestesses understood the mysteries that escaped the general public. Knowing the possibilities available to us when sacred sex and magick combine empowers our lives.

Men and women in the Web wrote this book to share common and uncommon knowledge about the magick of human sexuality. Magick and sex are sacred. Perhaps this book will give the entire aspect of sacred sexual priestesses in the Temples a different interpretation. Perhaps it will inspire people to discuss their own needs for magick and ecstasy. Perhaps it will create powerful spells that transform us or the world we live in. We envision big magick.

In this little book we discuss both our deep relationships in magick and sex and those in short-term energetic lovemaking. Both empower magick. Committed couples build a history together. They practice sex magick that takes great leaps of mindfulness into the universe and entwines with the Gods. They have time to work on intention, technique, and conscious merger. On the other hand, lovers who may not have long-term commitments use their joyous intercourse for magick in the here and now. As long as their communication is honest, *an it harm none*, they do as they will. We also know that individuals who have no human partners in sacred sex can work this magick in solitary, calling on the inner male and female to empower their intentions. Beyond that, many of us work with Spirit Lovers to experience a sexual sensual dynamic out of body. All of these experiences whether coupled, solitary or temporary work toward magickal ends.

In exploring sacred sex and magick, we seek individual transcendence and merger with the Divine. Our egos expand and lose their fear of annihilation. Our spirits embrace the essential soul of All Being, ours and the Other. One gateway to the Infinite is through sacred sex. We write this book to prop open that gate and invite you to enter. We expect to join forces with the Gods and Goddesses in this work. We hope you do too.

What is our collective experience? We all practice paganism, some for 30 years and one for a single year. We know the ethics and rituals for spell casting. We have learned to engage the chakras in lovemaking and carry that connection through orgasm. Sometimes we are better at that than other times. Sometimes we forget what we know. Many of us have been the priestesses drawing down the moon or the priests holding the energy in that ritual. We have drawn the Goddess and Gods into our bodies to speak to the community in inner court/outer court rituals. We are experts at grounding earth energy through our bodies and celestial energy through our hearts. We are skilled in chakra clearing. We are Reiki Masters. We are healers. Some of us are artists, musicians and writers. One or two studied tantra. Others studied yoga. One is an extraordinary channeler for extra-terrestrial and Native American guides. Several of us are mediums and readers. A few have kundalini Reiki attunements. Most of us are parents. Some are grandparents. Half of us have completed all four levels of Web Wicca training: *To Know the Magick, To Will the Magick, To Dare the Transformation* and *To Be Silent.* Most of us are shamanic healers and journey workers. All of us are spiritual teachers.

We think of ourselves as ordinary pagans. When we write down who we are and what we do, we realize the Web PATH Center has broad scope and deep training. Nevertheless, we are also human, annoying, distracted, and caught up in everyday life. Like everyone else, we work, pay bills, balance family demands, create art, wish we had more time, and work collectively to direct the Web PATH Center. We want all our readers to be encouraged. All pagans can create our lives as magickal, sensual experiences that heal and transform us and our world.

Introduction

What is Magick?

We understand magick to be an intentioned act designed to create a change. We create magickal change using connections across the worlds with the Gods, Goddesses, guides, spirits or elementals in order to make our desires physically real. Thus, magick is a physical and spiritual event. We voice our desires. We act out an appeal to our spiritual partners, we empower that appeal with ritual or spells and we receive what we asked for.

Is it that simple? No. Rarely is magick that straightforward. Sometimes we get what we asked for, but what we said wasn't what we meant. Sometimes out of kindness, our spiritual partners in magick refuse to return the goods. What we asked for would create more problems for us or for someone involved in the working. Other times our spiritual partners offer us something different or something more than we sought for the same reason.

For magick to work, we need to involve all of our selves. We have physical, emotional, mental, volitional, and spiritual bodies. Magick requires all of them. Not everyone creating strong magick identifies that as the process. The involvement of our whole self can be unconscious. Nevertheless, we are fully present on all levels when we make magick.

For most of us, magick happens when we do a seasonal ritual and the Goddess speaks. That is magick enough. Sometimes She speaks through us as in channeling, more magick yet. Magick ignites when we prepare a talisman, charm bag or other symbolic representation for the desired outcome and then empower it with spells. Magick happens when we mentally connect with the earth and make a compact for better weather, safety, or protection right on the spot. Magick happens when we form an intention with our brains, embrace it with our hearts and empower it with our will.

Some of the magick the writers of this book have worked protects old trees, the house and barn from severe weather. One spell produced $50,000 within two weeks of asking. Another released an old lover. One healed Electra, a very sick cat, overnight. Another used Reiki and cured the dog Oran's cancer over the weekend. At a Web healing seminar for people, a student brought in a sick puppy with liver failure who survived to live a full life. Every one of those events felt like a miracle.

Magick protects us. On a narrow road a car, tractor trailer, and bicycle passed each other when there clearly was not enough room, but the witches in the car sucked in their space. Magick helps us find things by saying 'reach.' We complete projects resisting our efforts by saying 'together.' Magick is practical.

Web members report spell workings that attract money and the means to make a business successful. Combined with divination, spell work indicates career choices. Our magick heals human illnesses too. Sometimes those health workings are combined with nutrition and physical therapy. One woman who relied on a walker three years ago, hikes small mountains now. Skin conditions, eye problems, chronic pain and respiratory illnesses have all given way to special healings. Some symptoms return because the lesson isn't complete, but all respond to the magick of energy healing.

We speak with the spirits; have relationships across time; and converse with plants and animals. Sometimes we make small magick. We manifest parking places in a crowded town or turn red lights green when that is important. We convince an ailing vehicle to make it home before it gives out. We run out of fuel as we coast into the gas station instead of miles down the highway. We set wards or weave protection around cars and houses so they are safe from thieves. Important letters cross country in a day instead of three. Space shrinks and time stretches when it absolutely must.

Magick is part of our daily lives. We chant spells for the

fertility of our gardens, crops and livestock. We call in the rain, or politely ask it to dwindle when there is too much water. We ask advice and inspiration for the fertility of thought when we embark on artistic crafts. We use dream work to solve problems our conscious mind stumbles over. We bless the work of our hands and the creativity of our minds. We can even become invisible, or at least unseen.

Several of us reconnected with soulmates in unexpected magickal ways. We make sense of our histories with past life memories and retrieve what we need to heal ourselves from old patterns that should have been buried long ago. We have discovered many of us shared common experiences in lives across the centuries. We use magick to disconnect wounded hearts from heart break, at the same time learning the lessons from those situations. We use magick responsibly and for joy. Magick also helps us connect in mind, spirit, and with others. With magick, we can send positive energies to help others, to protect them from negative energies or to send healing. Sometimes sending magick means remembering to bring a loaf of bread home.

As Willow Woman explains, magick is working with energy, that is to say frequencies or vibrations, in order to bring about change in our bodies, minds, hearts or spirits. Everything has frequency. Light, color, sound, music, radio waves, the chemical elements like gold, iron, or mercury, the compounds of salt or water, the mixtures like earth or air, the living beings of plants, animals, and the human body. All those things have energy signatures that fall within a range of frequencies and can be changed. When we intentionally manipulate the vibrational signature, magick can happen. That is half of the equation. The other half must be supplied by 'The All That Is'. That is why we call our magickal work with the Gods and Goddesses a partnership.

What is Sacred Sex?

For several of us, sacred sex may occur without intercourse or physical stimulation. Ritual grounding, raising the cone of power, drawing down the moon and holding the Gods and Goddesses within our bodies in ritual space all involve a rush of kundalini. This is sacred sex. As the Ditchwitch says, 'If, during cone of power raising you aren't feeling an ecstatic rush of orgasmic energy, you ain't doing it right.' The circle that shares the cone of power is part of a sacred orgasmic experience. Pegqua suggests that in ritual we are more focused on the magick than on the physical realities of sex, which may allow the sexual energy to rise through the body more freely.

In one ritual several years ago when we were calling Cerridwen and Cernuous, one of the younger women felt the God enter her as if she were sitting on his lap. Since that was an unspoken possibility, she had no context for the experience, but welcomed its arousal of both passion and power. She worked the ritual magick with him for the rest of the ceremony. When he was released from the circle, he took his withdrew from her, but I understand came back to her bed at night on other occasions. She was not leading the ritual nor taking a priestess role, but she is in fact a priestess as most of the Web women are.

Many of us have been indwelt by the Goddess during a moon ceremony. She has spoken through us as her channels. Our bodies thrum with divine sensuality when that happens. That resonance with the divine energy is available whenever we speak to the Gods and Goddesses, whether or not we intentionally draw them into humans standing at the altar. A lovely priestess among us turned into quite the coquette at a moon ritual she led, dancing and singing around the circle in what we all agreed was likely the most beautiful moon ritual we had ever seen. She had no memory of being flirtatious or sensual, thinking she only walked the circle. Similarly, when a group of us form the witches' mill in the center of the circle, right hands clasped over the cauldron as we walk deosil under the full moon, we speak prophecy. Sometimes it comes out in rhymed couplets, which rise up like an orgasm from our toes through our wombs and out of our mouths. We may or may not remember what we say.

On the other hand, for many of us sacred sex clearly involves intercourse that couples practice privately. The Web group emphasizes this magickal intention is conscious and agreed upon by both partners as they plan the spell and initiate their loving. Sacred sex is not casual, routine or forced. Intent is what makes it sacred. Spellworking is what makes it magick. We can experience this sacred sexuality from both an Eastern and Western approach.

From an Eastern perspective, sacred intercourse can involve the practice of tantra. When we allow our bodies to experience the rise of kundalini we open ourselves to expand our consciousness. We may experience the power of sensuality as a psychic orgasm which is not replicated with a physical release. When two people have the ability to take the sexual energy up the kundalini ladder through the chakras they are able to combine their power and reach levels higher yet in ecstatic experience. Sex magick is the practical use of that refined energy. It reaches beyond the rudiments of physical sex by working on a higher plane. It is a way of communicating at spiritual level not limited to life partners or married couples. Sacred sex in tantric practice requires a different head set to effectively reach those levels and practice them. A spouse may not be the one to partner transcendence.

From a Western perspective, sacred intercourse can also enact the Divine or Sacred Marriage known as the *hieros gamos*. This sacred intercourse joins the polarity of male and female in the two triangles of the six-pointed-star (hexagram) as one penetrates the other. These are equal triangles, so both penetrate each other as they slide together to make a star. We call this the Great Rite. We enact it with chalice and blade in public ritual, and privately with intercourse. However, the transformation involved in sacred sex creates energy of penetration and envelopment of one another so that it is not simply sexual intercourse. It is merger and connection on deep and magickal levels. We become each other and we become divine. As such, our will be done. That is magick for everyday life.

The priest and priestess enacting the Great Rite with the chalice and the blade, do their best to open themselves to the Divine and allow their bodies to feel the union/reunion of Divine and human, male and female, as they bring the symbols together. Sacred sex is the sacred union. It connects and reconnects individuals with the Divine Lover and with each other with intent. This power of connection exists whether the Great Rite is symbolic or physical. Our becoming and re-enacting the ecstatic union of God and Goddess, earth and sky or sun and moon, lights the spark of divinity within each of us.

It is also important to observe that the yin and yang of this rite are not necessarily male and female. Human gender is not the most important aspect of sacred sex. In nature when the intent is reproduction, organs that produce egg and sperm matter. If the creative impulse is magick of a different sort then the spark of passion plants the seed of an idea, the germination of an organization, or the creation of art apart from gender. Creation with sexual power is an inherent intent that is no less sacred if the partners are not nubile youths. Kundalini raised between people beyond child-bearing years or magick made between same sex partners is equal in its potential. Power ignited by priest and priestess in the sacred sex drama of the chalice and the blade draws fertility into ritual.

Make no mistake, intercourse and love are magick. They create an aura of peace, power, ecstasy, and merger that affects the wellbeing of the whole world. When we are able to open ourselves to perfect love and perfect trust we become one with the Divine. We allow the magick to happen with good intentions in mind. Then loving and helping neighbors and friends happens naturally. Intentional magick to create peace or transform lives can and does spread out from there. In all, our perspective and practice of sacred sex inspires us to look upon all life forms and their energies as sacred. All beings are deserving of our love because they are manifestations of the Divine. We are ALL sacred; there is far more than physical lovemaking to sex.

How Can Sex and Magick be Combined?

The word *intent* is bandied about frequently as people discuss magick, sacred sex, spells, charms and ritual. What is it we mean to create? Is a well-formed intent sufficient to combine power and desire in a constructive act of magick? Or is there something else involved in connecting heart, mind and will to manifest a desired outcome? Does sexual power make our magick more effective? Are there consistent and predictable ways to direct sacred sex to magickal intents? Simply stated, can we count on sex magick when we need it to work?

Yes we can.

In a group working when all are focused on an agreed outcome, say healing for a particular person in the hospital, then the poppet, talisman, candle or other representation of the ailing individual is placed centrally in the circle. We may have prepared it in advance, or created it there in sacred space during the ritual. Everyone works their expectation that the sick will recover fully. We each hold the magickal object, bless it and speak aloud our meaning for the healing spell so our intentions go into the symbol. Then we raise the cone of power over it to send that healing to the person in the hospital. Afterward we hold the symbol in our ritual space or take it to them.

How is this magick sexual? The cone of power is a rising of the kundalini through our bodies, which are in a state of arousal. They empower the charges that we make as we weave the spell energy together. As one woman said when we talked about how this worked after a ritual, 'You mean I just had sex with you all?'

Well, yes, but it was chaste. All was well. She was laughing. I never know what people know and what they don't, what they remember from classes and what they forget. Group work that is sent out with a sexual rush in a cone of power is sex magick. Otherwise we are waving our arms around and blowing smoke. Sometimes waving our arms in blind faith works. Magick is more apt to happen if we raise the power of the physical sensual body and charge our spells with passion and ecstasy.

Sex magick works individually. In a private working, couples might set up a healing ritual the same way we set up the group ritual and use the same intention. However, we would then engage in deep, sweet lovemaking, taking as much time as we have to raise the ecstasy, delay the orgasmic release while we visualize the spell, the healing and the rise of the energy created by our touches, kisses and caresses. As our arousal increases, so does the power of sex magick. Using our imagination, breath, or voice we draw it up through our bodies, through the nearby talisman and then out into the universe to ascend to Spirit, then descend into the body of the one who seeks healing. Sometimes we anoint the talisman with our sexual fluids, though we keep that poppet on our own altars.

Clearly it is important that we work this magick with the permission of the individual seeking healing. That is true whether or not we engage in physical lovemaking to empower the spell. We have had painful blow backs from instances where people tried to overrule the person who was in pain, 'for their own good, you understand.' A person who does not want healing energy should not be overruled. As they can refuse medical treatment, they can refuse magick. They are always in charge of their own bodies and what sort of healing they want.

To summarize, effective magick always involves ecstasy. Sex magick creates a spiritual rush of energy through the bodies of the people working magick. This rush is the kundalini and orgasm. A physical rising of sexual ecstasy between partners or among a ritual circle charges the spell and sends the magick on its way. In either case with our attention to the meaning and method of the ritual working it is sacred sex, ecstatic, orgasmic and strong magick. Yes, sex magick is reliable.

Chapter 1

Contemporary Paganism and Sex Magick: What is Going on Now?

Like any other magick, contemporary pagans engage in sex magick to extend their spiritual practice and alter their lives. Spells, merger with the Gods and Goddesses, expansion of consciousness, healing and ritual celebration are enhanced by sex magick. We are challenged to be aware that what we have been doing is sex magick. Our stories about sex magick make that clear. Then we examine the possibilities for contemporary paganism in exploring more applications for sex magick.

Sacred Sex and Personal Growth

Sex magick is an act of worship or divine connection. Even when we are not consciously drawing down the God or Goddess into our bodies and our lovemaking, they are present. The Sufi seer Rumi said, 'The way you make love is the way God will be with you.' In The Charge of the Goddess, Doreen Valiente wrote, 'Every act of love and pleasure are my rituals.' Sex magick is divine communication, prayer and worship. The Gods are present when we make love.

Satira, one of Web women who works regularly in trance and as a channeler related a shamanic vision in which she was in the Temple of Isis. The Goddess was seated on her throne and many of her devotees were present. Her son Horus was also there, looking as virile and handsome as one might expect, bronze skin, dark hair and eyes, chiseled features. Perhaps this was not the first time Satira had been to the Temple, but it was her first ecstatic connection with Horus. As the heat grew between them and he kissed her she felt the desire for him, but pulled back. They were not only in a public place, but in a Temple. His mother was watching, as were many of the others assembled in the hall. Raised in a nice comfortable Roman Catholic background where one does not have sex on the altar, part of Satira was horrified by his seduction. Part of her wanted him more than anything else in the world. He encouraged her. His mother nodded with approval and those around them smiled expectantly. As he removed her clothes and his, she found resistance fade. Then Isis encouraged her to enter the loving and called her, 'My daughter.' Satira gasped. Did that make her the sister of Horus? Did it matter? She was too far gone in the experience to care, and gave herself over to the ecstasy of embracing and enveloping the God in his mother's Temple as an act of worship.

That vision has never left Satira. It was a challenge of her beliefs about propriety in worship, about incest, about who the Gods are and what they believe. The encounter opened her to possibilities of divine and human relationships.

The truth is, we have Spirit Lovers waiting for us in Temples, wild places, even in our bedrooms. When we allow ourselves to transgress taboos foisted on us from a society that fears both sex and religion and is terrified of the Gods, then we learn who we really are, brothers and sisters of the Gods. We are co-creators. We are sons and daughters, but not always as children. We can grow up and be consorts, companions and friends. We are also lovers.

Anemone had a similar visionary experience. She appeared in a Hindu Temple and at the instruction of the Goddess exchanged places with her on a platform elevated above the crowd. The outpouring of love from the assembly was ecstatic, resonating her heart, womb and genitals. The two changed places many times, moving from the front row of worshipers to the raised area above them until the exchange began to feel natural. She was able to accept the adoration from the crowd and the Goddess. Only later did she realize most of those assembled in the Temple were Gods and Goddesses themselves, including Shiva who embraced his

Shakti in love and passion there in the midst of them all.

In that vision, the sacred sex was acted out in the Temple by a sacred couple. Anemone the seer was caught up in the energy of that deep loving. She also experienced the adoration given to the Gods as an ecstatic love showered on her. She broke through the sense of unworthiness to take her place freely on a pedestal. That elevation was not a comfortable place for her. It was a taboo as strong as the one against incest, but it was pierced and tattered in her vision.

This visionary sacred sex was brought to individuals to move them beyond their limiting beliefs. The values and behavior outside of the earth dimension are clearly different than those we live by here. There, familial relationships are not barriers to sexual encounters. We have heard that told in our ancient stories about the Gods and their many love affairs. The Isis story of loving one's brother who is sacrificed, birthing his child who becomes the father and repeating the cycle is part of our psychic legacy. We cannot understand the cycle of the rise of the vegetation God, his marriage and fertility offered for the fields and his subsequent sacrifice for the harvest if we apply our own moral codes to behavior from other worlds.

That is not to say we should change our laws and standards here in the earth dimension. Experiencing love with the Gods does not alter our marriage vows. We are not being offered models for this life in marrying our siblings or killing off sacrifices to enhance our harvests. These experiences and stories are meant to push our boundaries in love and extend our souls across the dimensions. We are more than we imagine in our souls and spirits. We are more than earth beings. When we operate in the world of spirit, we stop being limited human beings stuck in time and space. With that awareness of who we really are, we can return to the earth dimension, raise energy through our bodies and create great magick.

Sexual Healing through Ecstasy

Kerry Riley, in *Tantric Secrets for Men*, says, 'The single most important factor in lengthening life is to know the correct way to make love.' (p.191) Orgasm releases endorphins which heal us and lessen pain. Human touch and hugs held for a minute or two change blood pressure and respiration. We understand sex magick as a healing experience. Sex revitalizes us within. That rejuvenation is catching. It revitalizes people within our circle, even though we have no physical sexual connection together. It is magick by contagion.

Sex magick increases our understanding of the genders. By recognizing our own inner male and female, we build empathy and trust between the sexes which our society insists are at war. Diana Richardson, in *Tantric Orgasm for Women*, says, 'We must understand that woman is in fact half man and man is half woman.' (p.43) We understand sex magick creates communication and trust between partners. They may be same sexed or opposite sexed partners, but we all have a full spectrum of masculine and feminine within us.

Sex magick heals our sexual histories and dysfunction. It increases our self-love for imperfect bodies. Or should I say bodies that are perfect, but outside the societal norms? Broken hearts, fertility issues, and low self-esteem are well within the scope of sexual healing. Sexual obsessions, post-traumatic stress from sexual assault and other acts of violence, and fear of commitment, respond positively to sacred sex. Applying sexually charged magick to any of these life-limiting issues requires an understanding and loving partner. Alternatively our Spirit Lovers can work this magick with us when we are prepared to heal and ask them for help. The healing requires courage and creativity, but it works.

Connecting Across the Genders

As a beginning in sexual healing, we examine our own gender

identity and our notions about men, women and the intersexes. This is important because our pagan community includes people in traditional gender roles, feminist activists, heterosexual and homosexual couples, and individuals who have changed genders (intersexed). In the Web's introductory class, *To Know the Magick*, we typically journey through a hand-held mirror to meet our same sex and opposite sex selves. Men are often uncomfortable with their own femininity. Women may resist any suggestion of machismo in their personality. Intersexed and transgendered people find themselves confronted by more facets of being than they thought they had. These encounters are important initiations to the healing journeys to come. We start there because it is important to know who we really are. These other aspects of self are allies in our healing. They introduce us to other spirits. They are the Gods and Goddesses. They are also us.

How does this work? Our gender meditations occur in sacred space during an all-day seminar. The group grounds, breathes together and enters a guided meditation. First they are told to gaze into a mirror and connect to their deepest consciousness through their eyes. They hold this gaze long enough to feel a physical opening to the inner self. Then they are told to let the mirror enlarge or their bodies shrink so they can open the mirror like a door or sink through it like the surface of a pond. They enter the room on the other side of the mirror and visually explore it. Each person has a different experience at this point, so they are given time to understand where they are.

The next cue is for the students to see someone approaching through a door or corridor in the back of the room behind the mirror. This person is lit from behind, so initially their outline is all that is identifiable. The class is cued on whether or not this is the same or opposite sex self, so presumably the outline shows them the gender, though that is not always the case. The two approach one another curiously and are guided to make each other's acquaintance. They gaze into each other's eyes, observe each other's dress and appearance. Colors are important. They exchange names, gifts and secrets. When the encounter is complete they embrace, kiss and bid farewell. The alternative self then exits through the back of the room. The student returns to the mirror and climbs through to the ritual circle. They are cued to return to their normal size, to return the mirror to the normal size, breathe and look about to see where they are. Then they ground again. Students record this experience in their journals or Book of Shadows. We discuss the visions at length and then take a break before repeating the experience to meet the second self of the other sex.

When both journeys are complete, the students are encouraged to find an uninterrupted space of time once they get home, and make love to their same and opposite sex selves. They can meet in the same way through the mirror as long as they need to. Later such meetings will be more spontaneous and they can simply call one another. We include these aspects of ourselves in our daily routine and build relationships with our other selves to integrate them into our identity. In their private work, some people may include additional journeys to explore a wider range of gender possibilities since there are people who feel they inhabit the wrong sex body, people who were born with sexual characteristics that are ambiguous or inclusive of both male and female parts, and people who truly do not fit the societal sex roles. As a community, we seek to learn all we can about who we are and they are, and understand that we are all One. In the case of younger students who may not be exploring their bodies to stimulate orgasm, they are offered the option of going on a date with themselves, holding hands and kissing. The ecstatic merger will develop naturally as the teens explore their own sexuality in their own time.

Healing Applications of our Multiple Genders

We explore our gender identity to help us be more of who we are. Whether we are straight, gay, bisexual, transgendered or some other combination, the truth is that all potentialities reside in the many facets of our souls. However, we are all humans holding various levels of prejudice. We have erected boundaries where we need them. Sometimes those must remain intact. We learn biases where we are lazy in our unthinking, or fearful in our beliefs. We encourage people to confront prejudice and come clean about it. In the great breathtaking universe there is no room for distrust of an entire gender or sexual orientation. In a spiritual community, men may not mock or ridicule women. Women may not dismiss or belittle men. We welcome and celebrate the marriage or partnering of couples regardless of their genitalia. However, being human we all have history to work through, information to learn and stereotypes to unlearn. Working intimately with our same and opposite sex selves takes a big healing step toward those goals and does so with sacred sexuality.

We often refer to a plaque Anemone's grandmother had over the dining table about walking a mile in someone else's moccasins before criticizing their situation. All of us have a story about our own sexual initiation. All of us had sexual experiences that failed to live up to our dreams. All of us have our hearts broken at some time. Too many of us have been sexually abused or attacked. Where our pain hides our wounds within the body is as unique as our faces and physiques. Learning we have parts of our identity who share a gender role with those who wounded us is an important realization. We can learn more about men and how they think or women and how they intuit, as two examples, by connecting with the part of us that does the same left brain/right brain process. We may have thought that process was foreign to our own way of being, but it is not.

The good news is this lesson is fun! Meeting and loving

ourselves, drawing us both to ecstatic passionate orgasm is a joy. It is transformative and mind expanding. We learn to get over ourselves and be taught by the spirit. When we make love with our alternate selves, we set the scene with scented candles or flowers. Maybe we enjoy a picnic on the bed. We share favorite foods with our other self in our imagination, lick ice cream or juicy fruits off our own skin, and imagine sharing that. We sip some wine, play romantic music, or heavy metal rock if that's what turns us on. Maybe we watch a love story together as we woo ourselves as we wish to be wooed. We enjoy this connection in all ecstatic possibilities.

Healing Broken Hearts with Sacred Sex

Depending on whether or not a deep grieving heart is the result of a recent break up or an old hurt, the ecstasy of sacred sex can be with one's human lover or Spirit Lover. Obviously, if a divorce or betrayal has occurred, the last thing one should attempt is a sacred sex reunion. Sometimes we are grieving because a partner died. We think we will never be loved, never be sexual again. That is a time for the Spirit Lovers described earlier, or the Divine Lovers, to step in and work their magick by affirming our desirability. Knowing that our sex lives are not over because a relationship ended is healing in itself. Even when we feel hopeless, if we can organize our actions to create a romantic tryst with a Spirit Lover, our healing unfolds. Healing from loss is not a one-time event. This nurturing from spirit needs to continue until our hearts beat soundly and lovingly.

On the other hand, old unresolved wounds from the past step up to haunt us. Then an intentional tryst with our current human partner may work magick if we set the intent for healing. This requires both partners to be very patient with the process. It begins with talking. Actually all healing begins with talking. The wounded lover needs to tell his or her story to the healing lover. The listener needs to refrain from offering advice, fixes or even suggestions. Nods, hand holding, or reflective listening are helpful. These are affirmations that the speaker is being heard. When the story is done, the couple makes a magickal intent for healing the heart. They write it out together and place it on the altar near the bed. Perhaps they need to set up an altar in the bedroom if it isn't there already. For this ritual of sexual healing, they might need a black tourmaline to work through stuck places. That should be cleansed with salt water and placed on the altar.

They light incense for heart healing: rose, lavender, jasmine or neroli. They listen to music that vibrates the heart, maybe music that includes their special shared song. Then a loving sensual massage from the healing partner using oil that complements the incense works out the knots of tension. Long, slow, tender strokes reassure the wounded lover that this is a place of love and safety. As they continue the massage over the entire body, the healing partner reminds the other of their love, their promises to keep each other safe, their intention to release old pains and replace them with affection. The massage moves naturally into erotic caresses and kisses, which are returned according to the ability of the wounded partner to do so. If this begins as one-sided loving, that is part of the healing too. The healing partner always continues to protect the heart of the other, sending it gentle waves of love, softness and trust. Verbal communication of that intention is very helpful as the loving proceeds.

If the wounded partner cries, they both understand this is part of the release of old pain. The healing partner dries tears and murmurs words of encouragement. Merlin of the Web is the model for this. When we were offering weekly healing sessions he typically worked at the head of the client, while other healers worked with reflexology on hands and feet, acupressure along the meridians, and Reiki. He would often keep up a low hypnotic drone that reminded the client that he or she was in charge of the experience, that we would not offer anything beyond their comfort level, that we brought healing from the spirits, that the client was worthy of wellness, that they were loved, that they could love themselves and heal themselves. He frequently could not tell us what he intended to say beforehand, nor what he had said afterward. It was as if the Gods spoke their love through him.

Although it may be difficult to watch a loved one grieve and cry, this release is necessary. For the healing to work deep into the psyche, the healing lover holds and affirms the partner through all these emotional releases. Words help in encouraging the tears to wash out old pain. Affirmations of love and acceptance replace that pain and fill the gaps left as energy cysts leave the old wounds. Talking out loud about loving is sacred.

Unlike our group healing sessions, the private sexual healing between partners continues through sexual arousal to passionate and heated lovemaking, as long as the wounded partner is ready for that. Any grief that is stuck in his or her craw, unwilling to move, can be handled a couple of different ways. If the healing partner is skilled in extracting negative energy and general gunk from the aura and physical body, then with the partner's permission, that direct removal of old stagnant energy and its replacement with loving light is one option. The stagnant pain removed from the wounded partner should be thrown into fire or water, either real or psychic.

If the partner is not trained or confident in extractions, then the black tourmaline on the altar is useful in finding and releasing negativity, anger, and its inward correspondent depression. Either partner can hold the stone gently and meditate. Then they use it to scan the aura or chakras in search of where the blocking emotional pain is hidden. When the location makes itself clear by temperature, vibration, or intuition, then we hold the stone over that place and turn it slowly for short periods of time. Two or three applications are generally all one does at one healing session. We consciously draw the negativity into the tourmaline as if winding it inside. When the area is cleared, the stone is returned to the altar or placed in a bowl of water. Later, we cleanse the stone in salt water after it is used in this way.

Once the energy clearing is complete, the heart and body of both parties is usually open to the rest of the sacred sexual experience. Their bodies return to arousal, kissing and caressing until they both desire one another. The most healing sexual exchange involves penetration and envelopment; we use both terms to acknowledge the polarity of sex. The use of the term penetration by itself is charged with a history of possessing a lover instead of merging bodies and spirits. Sexual healing works through that old history and reframes our lovemaking into a sacred tryst of equals by including envelopment with penetration. Speaking plainly, in traditional intercourse between a heterosexual couple, he penetrates her, but in that act finds himself enveloped by her soft and juicy folds. One is equal to the other. Alternate sexual practices such as oral sex or the use of sex toys can include penetration and envelopment – moving our mental image of sexuality to include both penetration and envelopment as *equally* important in healing. It is also a very stimulating picture. However, other orgasmic experiences or non-orgasmic tantra are also effective, depending on the couple's preference.

The couple may continue to reinforce this healing during the following week by sitting close together each with their sending hand placed on their partner's chest between the breasts over the heart, naked or clothed. Through their hands, they send pink light for love. They also send healing and acceptance of the lover. What follows is up to them.

Other Emotional or Physical Healings
We can address other concerns using the same approach changed to fit the problem. Sexual dysfunction or pre-orgasmic situations

in which one partner cannot feel their arousal or climax in the body could respond to a healing session similar to the one described above. If energy blocks can be located that free the sexual responses and connection to the brain, which is our most important sex organ, then they are removed the same way as the other wounds, either with energy extraction or by the black tourmaline. A rosy pink rhodochrosite placed over the heart or pubis is very effective at creating positive sensual and healed energy responses in place of the blocked ones. Roses or rose scent are also helpful.

Healing sexual dysfunction often deals with shame in one form or another. Shame about appearance, shame about sexual history, shame about being a sexual person. Sometimes we need to start this sacred healing as a solitary. We live in an odd culture in which the wonderful word vagina has become unacceptable. Simple images of artistic vaginas are removed from Facebook as if they were pornographic. Think Georgia O'Keefe flowers. They are beautiful and arousing, but not indecent. There is an increase in plastic surgery used to re-size women's labia to look more pubescent because voluptuous labia are ridiculed. Similarly, men still feel shame if their penises do not measure up to mythic proportions of porn stars and stallions. Sexual dysfunction that is rooted in negative feelings about one's body can respond to love and appreciation from the soul who lives in that body.

Let's all assume we could make a list of things we don't like about our bodies. To turn that around, we can begin our day by gently caressing ourselves head to toe. We run our fingers through our hair and sensually appreciate it without criticism. If our hair has disappeared, then we appreciate the sensation of our smooth heads. The idea is to love the feeling of it. Then we proceed to caress our faces, necks, shoulders, on down the body including the breasts, nipples and genitals all the way to our feet. We can do this every day as we shower, but not with a wash cloth. The idea is to feel the body with our fingers and hands, and for the body to feel their caresses. Similarly, we can do this if we apply body lotion, caressing the body first without the lubricant is better than after it is all oiled up. We want to truly feel our skin. We send love and acceptance to all our parts as we do this. We think about how well our parts work, what we like about them and are grateful.

When we have pain or illness in some parts of our body, we send even more love in the form of light and warmth. People often miss the fact that illness is a message to our consciousness from our bodies that something needs attention. Medical attention is impersonal and off-putting much of the time. That painful body part craves love. Our instinct may be to reject or resent our illness. We label hurting parts bad knees or bad backs, as if they did something wrong. Instead, embracing and loving the joint or muscle that hurts can enhance the medical healing available from our doctors.

All of this is connected to sacred sexuality because touching, loving, accepting our bodies is sensual. When we engage in a full body caress, the kundalini is awakened. Our energy meridians respond by sending currents up from our souls to our genitals and then to heart and brain. Practiced every day, and then shared with a partner these techniques can open up one's sexuality and reconnect our awareness and brain to the rest of our body.

Sacred sex and magick can also heal or improve ob/gyn problems and conception issues at least as often as over the counter medication or some medical interventions. Painful periods respond to the body caresses. Acupressure routines diminish pain and cramping. They can relieve constipation and bloating that go with dysmenorrhea. When women reach menopause, meditation and connection with the dark Goddesses can include sacred sex in the same way it is included with the same-sex selves. Bringing the body/mind into harmony with the crone Goddesses and conducting a croning ceremony resolves many of the usual complaints of hot flashes, temperamental outbursts and general misery we are warned about.

Does sacred sex and appreciation of one's body answer low sex drive and low testosterone in men? We don't have any anecdotal evidence on that. If loving one's body and engaging in positive affirming sexual encounters with one's partner and with the spirits helps women, it should work with men. In any event, experimenting with the process is healthy and fun. There are acupressure routines to include for a waning sex drive and erectile dysfunction.

In the case of people undergoing fertility treatments, adding sacred lovemaking can take away the physical pressure to perform on the schedule of the fertility cycle. The joy of finding each other through touch, caresses, penetration and envelopment can encourage eggs and sperm and improve their ability to find each other because joy has an energy signature that affects everything.

How Sacred Sex Can be Used in Contemporary Paganism

The possibilities are limited only by our imagination. Once we have relearned to love our bodies, we can engage in orgasmic healing for ourselves and each other. We can change our body/mind response to sexual stimulation by allowing the good feelings to infuse the entire body. We can live more comfortably with our physical cycles. We can accept and continue to love our changing bodies as we mature and age. We can improve our own relationships. We can resolve old wounds and fears picked up from our past. We can deepen our rapport with the Gods.

We can use the power of that love and ecstasy to forgive people who behaved badly so they stop taking up space in our heads. We can move on and release our obsession with old lovers. We can reach out and reconnect with fragments of our souls that took off without us rather than live through harmful events in negative environments. They will be very attracted to the positive sensual place we are creating for ourselves within sacred sexuality. We will be more sensitive, more sensual and more attractive because of that. When we live alone and are in love with our own bodies, we find we are not alone long.

Intentional Sex and Healing

Intentional sex involves the magick of honesty and openness with our partner to co-create healing of past traumas. This process requires integrity and honor so together we have a clear vision of what will be brought about through lovemaking. The vision evolves and grows with the relationship. The conversation continues throughout.

What Does One Manifest Through Sexuality Other Than Child Bearing?

Intentional sex is an inward fertility, a ripeness of spirit that two people nurture together. Spiritual and emotional bodies continuously bear fruit by working on different aspects of self from embryo through birth and growth. For example, a couple who embark on healing may create the spark of their magic through intentional sex. The power of love and orgasm continues to nurture healing between them. When it is mature and ready to be born, the healer persona emerges from the inside out so that the whole word can see it. Not only have they healed their own trauma in a maturing relationship, they are prepared to offer physical healing, counsel or ritual to others, albeit not usually in a sexual manner. The initiation and education of a healer started intimately and grew in the physical, emotional and spiritual bodies in the same way dis-ease took root. When completed, the soul is healthy, the body in balance and others benefit through Reiki or other modalities the couple chose to learn.

Other examples of the inner fertility may be the magic of a creative life in the arts. The creative urge is healed from self-doubt, procrastination, obsessive criticism, compulsive revision and fear. Performance, visual arts, music or completed books are born from the creative spark two people initiate in their love. The Web has a shared value that spiritual ecstasy, sexual orgasm and the arts all work with the same energy. The rush and joy are the same.

Similar applications of intentional sex can be made to building and construction, gardening, food production, career development, travel and the rest of life's riches. Intentionally beginning a project shared between lovers in their erotic connection then nurturing it the same way creates powerful change and evolution. It makes life work. However, a creative force like this needs conscious direction or the unconscious will act on its own. The body's default creativity is pregnancy. Intentional child bearing is ideal. That includes the couple's manifestation of what a child needs: a home, stability, adequate finances, education, self-esteem, love, security and confident parents who can provide those things.

Shawn Marie reminds us that our personal history influences how the conscious and unconscious line-up. We start out wanting a relationship without dealing with our personal hang-ups. If we are closed off and unable to deal honestly with our lovers, our emotional bodies leave us with sex that is unfulfilling or guilt ridden because we were dishonest. She took a time out from relationships so she could understand herself. Self-loving needed to be an important part of her self-approval. Now she carries her love with her through arts, tattoos, healing work, and parenting so the intentions she birthed with herself are more than physical or emotional responses. They are magick from the will and they are spiritual.

She says that during time out from relationships, the artistic fruit is fueled by physical intimacy with the self. Learning what orgasm is without being over critical of past choices or body image is important. She, like many of us, had not selected partners interested in walking a joint path. We can all be self-absorbed using sexual encounters as joy rides. Intentional sexuality and its magic require we talk with the one person who really matters, instead of everyone else. As a single mom, she is learning not to be a control freak in bed or out. Relinquishing control or leadership to another person is difficult. However, thinking only we can please ourselves is unhealthy. Intentional sex shares with another what is pleasuring and creates orgasm. Together we choose what life priorities we empower through sex. Consciously working through any barriers that prevent us from this level of communication is essential.

People without partners can experience intentional creativity through self-pleasuring and honesty with themselves. Telling our souls the truth about us is no easier than telling someone else. If we wish to heal sexual or emotional trauma with orgasm and caresses, then we tell ourselves what happened. We place it in the past and realize it is no longer happening. We may use spell magic and burn the symbols of the past on the bedroom altar. Then we intentionally create our healing from the spark of conception through birthing our healed self. This is a project that can take nine months. It is important not to rush into believing too quickly that it is done with. We must be impeccable with our word (Don Miguel Ruiz, *The Four Agreements*).

In creating a magical relationship with intentional sex, Shawn Marie advises we be gentle with ourselves. Give it time. Honest relationships are not found in the movies and TV. Our media examples are inaccurate. Don't measure against them. For her the magic is about communication and openness, not ritual or spell work. However, what comes out of that is indeed magical.

Chapter 2

Contemporary Paganism: How is Sacred Sex Used in Ritual?

Much of the sexuality we experience in ritual goes unrecognized. Pagans don't warn people that they will experience sexual feelings as a matter of course in ritual and magick for fear of shocking them. Maybe some think those feelings are so obvious they can remain unspoken. Others may dampen them or numb themselves to a rush of ecstasy in public and so ignore that sacred sexuality is present in common pagan rituals. Furthermore, people expect children to have no sexual feelings, so any activity to the contrary is deemed inappropriate. Should children be involved if practicing paganism includes sexual feelings?

Biologically, children have sexual feelings in the womb and after they are born. They think nothing is out of the ordinary when grounding creates pleasant sensations within unless the adults in their lives, as often happens, introduce shame about their natural feelings. There is no reason why children should not learn how to direct earth energy through them from earth to sky and be taught about this rush of life force in language appropriate to their age. Likewise, visitors and strangers can identify the energy moving through them as love or relaxation without confronting the fact that kundalini and orgasm are part of the ritual process.

Grounding

The first part of the any ritual, including committee meetings and art work, begins with grounding. The last part is a release of the grounding. We can use a variety of guided meditations to connect our energy to the earth: trees, rocks, and plants are common images. In each case, we draw the earth energy into our bodies, pulling it up the spine and out of the crown of the head. Moving the earth energy through the body encourages the release of kundalini. A full grounding connection includes the mind and body. A rush of sexual arousal is normal. Its presence is a signal that one has truly hooked up with Gaia, the tree dryads or the rock people. Anemone tells Web students that grounding is the most important thing she has to teach them. In this brief tree meditation based on Starhawk's model in *The Spiral Dance* we demonstrate the ecstatic possibility of grounding.

Grounding Meditation

Sit quietly and be still in your body with your feet on the floor. Breathe deeply into your middle to relax. Feel your root chakra, genitals, belly and thighs relax and open. This occurs naturally when you center and breathe into your womb place. Man or woman, it is the same.

Imagine that you are a tree. Your torso is the trunk. Your arms are the branches; your fingers the twigs and leaves. Feel them shift into flexible wood swaying in a psychic breeze. Then breathe down your spine knowing it is a kundalini channel to your seat of being. Feel this relaxation in your mouth, breasts, heart and lungs. You open to the experience. As your body tingles, send roots out of your tail bone into the earth. Your roots move easily outward to penetrate the earth. Feel the caress of the earth as they descend to the bed rock, deeper and deeper into the earth. Touch the bedrock and know this is the bones of Gaia. Your root hairs cross the rock to attach to the rough surface. You and Gaia connect and exchange loving energy through these rootlets.

Send your love down to the rock with your breath. Draw her compassion up to your spine as a tree draws water and nutrients. As that earthy passion arrives, let it infuse your body down to the toes and up to the crown. Think about each part of you and let the connection sink in. When your tree is filled with Gaia's love, let it spout out of your head like a fountain and fall back over your skin in a sensuous bath. Gaia soaks in this love as it drips off your skin. She sends it back through your roots to cycle through both of you again and again. You are filled with earth energy, stabilized, strong and well. Hold this awareness throughout the ritual.

In the process of this grounding, you likely felt a rush or tingle move from the earth through your genitals and up your spine. Encourage it. Revel in it. This high level energy is what we make magick with. Rather than cast a circle or empower a spell with our vitality, we work with the energy of the earth. When the magickal working is complete, we release the energy we gathered in a similar way, working backward. Sometimes we place our hands on the ground to do this.

Grounding Release Meditation

Again be still in your body. Breathe deeply as before, first as a cleansing breath and then as a centering breath. Feel the rise of power from the root chakra and genitals through the heart and to the head. It has been there all the time during your work. Assess your physical being. Find any spots that seem too still, achy or buzzy. Balance these spots by moving the love held from Gaia around your body until you feel the same, back to front, top to bottom, right to left. Then deliberately slow the fountain in your crown so the stream of excess power falls back into your skull and down your spine from the head, chest, torso, all the way down to the genitals and root chakra. Always keep what you need for good health. Pull the excess energy up from the toes to the base of your spine. Feed the collected power down your roots to the bedrock. Feel your body return to normal; the kundalini link fades. Ask Gaia to receive this energy to use as she will, to heal the earth, to strengthen her core or create new land. You are nourishing the earth with love as she nourished you. Do this with reverence and gratitude. Breathe into your center and come back to your ordinary awareness.

Dance and Ritual

Movement and music open the energy centers and enhance the sensuality of love and ritual. In Wicca III we dance the elements as a meditation, moving to music in order to experience earth, air, fire and water from inside out. Belly dancing, yoga, and hula all open the pelvis and loosen the sacrum. Concentrating on hips and genitals as we move creates a connection to the earth and allows deeper grounding through the whole spine, neck and brain. Ritual and sacred sensuality is a full-bodied experience encouraged by sinuous movement.

Begin the connection to our ecstatic bodies. Stand and weave a figure of eight with your hips, thinking of the symbol being drawn in the air by your genitals. Consciously extend that symbol downward to trace itself on the ground between your feet. Visualize it. Be aware of how that spreads through your body. Accept and enjoy that energy. Experience it as communication between the physical and the spiritual. Then address each of the four directions with body movements designed to entice them into your circle.

In the east your movements are like the wind. Experiment with the light breeze and the strong storm. Twirl and welcome the wind, keeping in mind the weaving of energy through your hips. Call the sylphs of the air and fly with them around your circle.

In the south dance with the high energy of fire, leaping like flames and smoldering like banked coals. Draw the heat into your body and send it back again. Feel your joints soften and open with the melting fire. Welcome the power of the djinn to your circle and be amazed.

In the west dance with the rhythm of the waves, ebbing and flowing like a tide. Float on the surface of the water, sink deep into its embrace and know you can breathe like the merfolk.

Undulate. Let the kundalini ripple up your spine as you articulate your vertebrae. Let the water wash away stiffness and inhibition so you can be free through your sacrum. Feel the mounting arousal as the undines join your circle.

Then turn back to the earth and trace infinity on her face. Feel the strength of the great stones in your legs and feet. Root yourself and sway your hips in tune with Gaia's dance as you call the gnomes in from beneath the earth through her caves. Welcome the earth energy within your inner spaces. You may wish to embrace the ground and lie still, listening for her heart. You have opened your mental, emotional, magical and physical bodies with dance and connected them with the elementals.

All nature emulates the passion and heat of dance. The Ditchwitch tells this story as a voyeur of nature:

The lover approaches her, cautious, yet eager. She beckons, her silken strands floating, glistening in the dim light. I stand and stare, transfixed with the awe of what I am witnessing. I dare not get too close; I do not want them to be aware of my presence and leave before they have finished their tryst.

He strides across the bridge of silken steel, faster now. His whole life has led to this moment. They reach towards one another. They touch with a gentle push against each other, caressing, melding, pulsating with eagerness as they begin their dance. She twirls her silks, he cannot resist her sexual urgency and responds as she wishes. Together, still touching, they bob and weave, in unison, each a mirror of the other. They are a perfect union, Nature's instinct embodied as the need, the desire to co-create is their master. In obvious ecstasy, they are as unaware of me as I am so totally aware of their desire and pleasure. I silently bid them farewell, and leave the Golden Orb Spiders to their night of sexual surrender.

In our private moments, we dance for our lovers. We dance with our lovers. We create passion with our swaying. We intensify the magic with the body.

Cone of Power

Being grounded and in touch with the elementals means the root chakra is open and receptive. Performing spell work or healing magick in a well-grounded state will cause blood to flow to the genitals. That energy is then channeled to the spell or healing by envisioning a spiraling cone of psychic power moving from our bodies around the circle through the elementals to the target. When we raise a cone of power, the energy rises through us from the earth starting at the root chakra, through the genitals, up the spine through the heart and out the head and hands to the intended goal. This is a sexual rush.

But how do we create an effective cone of power? What is it? Frankly, not everyone who helps raise this energy needs to understand it, but someone does. New people and children can imagine this as a swirling external energy raised by chanting, singing or dance that peaks overhead and is sent off by the breath or shout from the group. They may see us then catch the returning energy and place it in the spell, but they likely think we are simply acting out a drama. That is exactly what they are supposed to think. For the trained or initiated celebrants standing in a circle, raising energy from the earth through their bodies in an orgasmic release of snaking kundalini is a stronger sending.

Our Visualization

We begin with a focus on where our feet connect to the earth. We imagine a direct link if we are indoors, as if the building is no barrier between our feet and the earth. We invite the energy of Gaia to rise in our bodies through the feet and legs, up to the genitals in the root and belly chakras. That includes the vagina, labia, clitoris, womb and ovaries for women; the penis, testicles, vas deferens, and prostate gland for men. Men may wish to

41

include the space behind the testicles, which is very erogenous. It is analogous to the vagina and labia. There is even a little line there as if it were a seam where the vagina might have been. They may also wish to include that interior space in the lower belly that we reference as the *womb place*. Remember we are all both male and female. Our bodies hold the potentiality in them. We encourage research for folks who have an unclear vision of their anatomy.

The energy continues to rise in two channels up the spine, winding like a DNA spiral that meets and crosses at each chakra. We hold this feeling in our bodies as it increases our arousal and internal power. Because most images of this are two-dimensional, people tend to think of these arcs as flat crisscrossing lines. They aren't. The DNA molecule and the rising kundalini are three dimensional images that actually spiral around the body as they ascend through us, thus the name 'cone of power'. At Yule, there are popular yard decorations made of a spiral of lights configured to resemble a fir tree. A person could stand in the middle. We visualize a full spiraling cone of power with the lines of light spiraling both deosil and widdershins, in around and through our bodies.

The lines of power then rise up through the body and cross at the belly, the stomach, the heart, the throat, the brow and the crown and then shoot up through the transpersonal point above the head. At the transpersonal point, the cone becomes a straight cord of power, which joins the other cords from the circle and continues up into the ether as if shot from an arrow. It arcs and returns to the earth at the location where the magick is taking place.

That location could be the altar where the magick started in order to empower a poppet or other talisman. The energy can enter a person receiving healing or other intervention. In those cases, the celebrants touch the talisman or recipient as the energy returns. In a large crowd, all gesture toward the poppet or individual. Some prefer pointing the magickal index finger of the sending hand at the recipient; others prefer using their wands. A third and effective way is to reach out toward the recipient with both hands, the thumbs and index fingers making a triangle through which the returning power condenses and flows into the charged object of magick. Not everyone needs to gesture in the same way, depending on the circle's own traditions.

Alternatively, the cone of power can arc and enter someone or something far distant for healing or transformation. In that case, the gesture is sent first straight up toward the stars and celestial beings who are blessing the energy raised by the circle and then moves toward the geographic location the group has identified. For example, if the circle is sending healing for someone in hospital located miles west of where they meet, then everyone turns to the west with their gesture and visualizes the person receiving the healing energy.

What is the sender's ecstatic sensation of infusing the recipient with powerful magick? The sexual energy increases as the cone of power builds. The energy release out of the crown and through the transpersonal point is like an orgasm, which may continue as the cone arcs and then shatters internally as the rocket returns to earth. The pause and then arcing of the cone back to earth releases the energy which may well continue to throb until it settles much more gently into the recipient. The sender needs to ground and reconnect with the earth until the chakras and physical body have calmed back to their normal state. What does the human recipient feel? Perhaps nothing. Perhaps a tingling warmth, a sudden rush like a psychic summer breeze, perhaps a thrumming like musical rhythms from a distance, or the blessing of deep compassion and love. The energy is stepped down by the celestials to flow compatibly with the recipient and bless them at a level that is healthful. In hands-on-healing we do the same. We work with our guides to blend our energy so it is soothing and within the spectrum the people receiving healing can accept.

But wait, there is more. A cone of power is effective if the majority of people in the circle can share the described visualization. It is more effective if the leader and perhaps others can add sacred geometry to sacred sex in their visualization. The Golden Mean or ratio of 1:6 known as *phi* resonates with our bodies because we are built on the same ratio. Da Vinci's Vitruvian Man spreads out his arms and legs in a perfect circle. He embodies the *phi* proportions from fingers to hand, hand to arm, arm to torso and so on. Ideally there are six finger lengths to an arm; six head lengths to our height. The mathematical spiral associated with the Golden Mean mirrors the spiral of energy raised with the cone of power. It follows Fibonacci's progression of 0+1=1; 1+1=2; 1+2=3; 2+3=5. Without going into the mathematics of it all, concentrate on the truth that what is past plus what is present equals what will be. The events that have passed plus the magick of the circle creates the new outcome. Magick transforms in an organic fashion that connects reality with the possibilities.

To accomplish this, the priestess mentally gathers her kundalini spiral to the one next to her. Then she takes the sum of their ecstasy and adds it to the next person. She gathers the energy of all three of them and adds it to the fourth person and so on all around the circle. At the high point of a magickal working the priestess weaves the circle's energy into a collective circle and sends it out into the universe or down into a talisman as described above. Each person creates the spiral of energy within. The priestess weaves the energy offered by each participant into a larger spiral, which winds inward from the edge of the circle toward the center in the same way the spiral dance winds inward. The cone of power then ascends in a spiral upward, often sent out with a group gesture of raised hands to be caught by the deities and directed to the recipient of the magickal working. Led with intention and skill, the celebrants may feel the cone build, grow and launch in the same way they feel the kundalini rise within their own bodies. If that escapes the notice of people standing in the circle, then the priestess who leads the cone should be the one to see and experience the greater group's weaving. If she does, there will be no question of when to release the cone, when to peak the humming, chanting or dance used to raise the energy and when to catch the energy on its return in order to send it into the recipient.

Many times the cone of power is raised and released to the universe without paying attention to where it lands. We often lack any awareness that this energy arcs and goes somewhere. In fact, the celestials catch it and send it back blessed, shaped and empowered to do the work we desired using the same magickal progression. They add our kundalini to theirs. They can make up for our lack of attention, but partnering with them to complete the magick is a powerful act. Our partners in magick are the Gods and Goddesses, our ancestors, our guides, or the Universal All Being. Who our partners are depends on who we called to the circle and who has an interest in the work we do. Our sensual sacred sexual energy is raised and joined with theirs to create real magick.

Drawing Down the Moon

A ritual invoking any deity into the body of the priestess or priest is apt to arouse sexual heat because they are spirits and we are bodies. Our merging with them is euphoric. Evoking them into the circle as witness to our rites will, at times, create a similar sexual arousal as they acknowledge us individually. We make a distinction between invoking or drawing the deities into our bodies and evoking or calling them into our circle. Drawing down the moon is one occasion when we celebrate the full invocation of the lunar Goddess into the priestess. From her the Goddess may also move to indwell others in the circle.

Because this is a sexually ecstatic rite, we do not share full

45

invocation or drawing down on sexually inexperienced people. However, when we celebrate a full moon ceremony in which we bring the lunar Goddess into the priestess and from her into other divinely selected priestesses, then that ecstasy runs through the priestesses. Their joy impacts all of those assembled and safely raises energy in each of us. Admittedly the rush of passion is one reason to hold such a ritual.

Other reasons include:

- Oracular prophecy and information from the lunar Goddess through her priestess;
- Love and worship of the Goddess and enjoyment of her presence;
- Growth and personal development from the teachings of the lunar Goddess;
- Weaving, merger and binding of our auras with one another and with the Goddess.

Similarly, if we conduct a sun ritual we draw the solar God into the priest. Occasionally we hold an inner court/outer court ritual in which the sacred couple is drawn into a priestess and priest who receive the celebrants one by one in a separate room. The celebrant is free to ask a question, request a boon or favor, or simply offer thanks and gratitude for blessings received. The God and Goddess speak through their channels and offer what they will.

There are many ways to call the Goddess into the priestess or the God into a priest. Gardnerian and Alexandrian Wiccans use the five-fold kiss. The Web PATH Center has an adaptation of that, not wishing to claim affiliation where there is none. The five-fold kiss draws the presence of the Divine into the human from the feet, knees, womb/womb place/phallus, heart/breasts and lips. The couple embraces chakra to chakra, feet slipped between each other's feet as they kiss their lips. When this is completed with love and openness, the sexual energy rises in all of us.

Alternatively, the priestess or priest can raise their arms in the chalice position and call the Goddess into their own bodies. On the other hand, their partnering ritual leader can call the deities and then gesture down the body with wand or athame to welcome the deity who then descends through the body. Satira and other channelers close their eyes to journey inward while calling to the Goddess who then arrives as she will. However the invocation is done, the Goddess is actually present in the priestess. The channeler may or may not remember the words spoken when the ritual is finished.

In most of our moon ceremonies, the priestess holding the presence of the Goddess walks the circle looking into the eyes of the women in the circle. She chooses a few to join her in the center of the circle. With words, gesture, or a sacred kiss the Goddess shares her presence with each of them. The priestesses then walk around a center altar or around a cauldron. Meanwhile, the men and other women consciously hold protective energy and strengthen the circle for them. The priestess may join right hands over the center in a witches' mill. Eventually one will speak and the others follow. They do not sound like themselves. Their words and voices are changed to fit the Goddess. The rite finds a natural conclusion when the truth has been spoken. Then the Goddess is released with a reverse gesture or phrase, first by the lead ritualist to her supporting priestesses and then by the priest of his partner priestess. (We avoid the term high priestess.) The supporting men from the circle bring food and drink prepared for the occasion in order to help ground the women who served the Goddess. The food is shared around the circle with all of the assembly. This is followed by hugs and kisses of love and gratitude. The energy runs high. Couples often make an early night of it so they can finish the working privately.

Pegqua shared her experience with drawing down the moon. She reminded us it is best to enter a ritual with no expectations because our experience will be much deeper. Expectations limit us and the magick.

She writes:

I had participated in drawing down the moon as part of the outer circle holding the energy, but never in the inner circle until Wicca III. Our teacher was ill and asked me to take her place. I was very unsure, but because she believed in me I agreed. I heard murmurs among the class: 'Why would she pick her?' 'I would be a better choice!' Trust me that didn't help my worry. But I meditated, hot tubbed and prepared myself.

We were lined up to attend circle when our priest Merlin drew me back, looked in my eyes and gave me a kiss. Then I knew it would be as it should. When the time came to draw the Moon Goddess into me I could feel her descend through my chakras and arouse all my senses very much like sexual arousal. I felt we were in harmony. When I circled to find my fellow priestesses she picked them (including the naysayers). When we delivered the Goddess's message we were in complete harmony. I chanced a glance into the cauldron and saw her face smiling back at me.

The whole time I could feel my anchor Merlin's holding power as well as the outer circle. After the ritual when the Goddess was released from me it was as powerful as an orgasm. Until that experience I would never have considered group sex, but that ritual showed me the incredible power that could be harnessed and directed. No, I haven't tried that, but I believe that in drawing down the moon, we are harnessing the same communal power.

The Great Rite in Ritual

As we have said previously, the Great Rite is a symbolic ritual that mirrors the sacred marriage of the Gods. When we wish to include that dynamic in our group rituals, the ritualists draw the presence of the Divine into each other. Then with eyes locked, they hold the chalice and blade aloft. Slowly one lowers the blade into the chalice while drawing the Divine energy through the chakras system and through the athame into the chalice. The other holding the chalice opens the chakras and receives that energy on behalf of the circle and the earth. This ritual is included in rites that celebrate fertility, such as Beltane and Samhain. Within our story of the wheel of the year, the Goddess is impregnated at these sabbats. In May she conceives the harvest to be enjoyed all summer and fall. In October she conceives the new Sun King to be born at Yule. There are other ways to understand the wheel of the year. Those are our lynch pins of fertility rites at the Web.

The Great Rite empowers handfastings, efforts at conception, new creative endeavors, moon rituals, and other celebrations of fertility. It can also bless initiation, although we have not used it in that way. We have not hesitated to perform the rite when children and families are present, as they often are at the Web. The symbolism goes over the heads of the youngsters. Teenagers may be embarrassed when it is their parents performing the rite. In kindness, we let them know well ahead of time so they can sit this ritual out if they wish.

We seek a healing application in fertility rituals. The symbolic Great Rite performed by ritualists who have activated their own inner sexual identities can provide the same energy as orgasmic intercourse. In a group made up of people who have learned to direct their own kundalini energy, the group mind can meditatively raise the same or similar energy to charge the cone of power directed to fertility and sex magick.

For example, the Great Rite added to moon rituals at different phases can be applied to healing dysmenorrhea (the new moon); infertility, ovarian cysts, sexual dysfunction (full moon) or menopause and aging (dark moon). We set up a ritual similar to the healing ritual discussed above in the section about the cone of power. Because we are working in public with families, we include the symbolic Great Rite to increase the rise of the kundalini and then direct the energy to the healing poppet or talisman.

Similarly, we can work gardening and agricultural magick in ways that include the Great Rite. We bring plants, seedlings, seeds, or other representation of our gardens and fields to the ritual altar. We enact the Great Rite before the altar and then raise the cone of power over our garden dreams, catching it as it returns back from the Gods blessed and more fertile than before. Then we gesture with wand, index finger, or a sacred triangle made with thumbs and forefingers to infuse the garden plants and seeds with our fertility spell. Then we take our seeds and plants home for our gardens to work magick by contagion with all the rest of the food we plant. We might also bring a pot of soil from a field that has been abused by modern farming methods. We feed it earth worms and then return it to the soil to begin an organic reclamation once we have celebrated the Great Rite and enhanced it with the cone of power.

Anemone recommends a chant sung to her garden as she planted tomatoes, peas, beans, and carrots: *'Grow little plants, and seeds of the fields, bring to us bounteous harvest and yield.'*

Whatever the magick being worked, we need a representation of the desired outcome on the altar. Couples seeking conception might place baby pictures or booties on the altar. Homemade booties made ritually with the love and desire for a child crocheted into them are strong talisman to call a soul to a womb. The talisman is presented to the four directions. In the north, we ask the blessings of the earth on the body of the child and mother and father. In the east we ask the blessing of the air on the mind and vision of the child and mother and father. In the south we ask for strength of will and creativity (conception) from the fire for the three of them. In the west we bring love to the family and wrap them in peace and compassion from the waters. Then we enact the Great Rite using the chalice and blade of the prospective parents, raise a cone of power, send it out to the Gods and Goddesses chosen by the couple, and bring it back to be earthed in the chalice and the blade. We close the rite and open the circle in our usual practice, and send them home with good wishes.

The possibilities for magick empowered by both the Great Rite and the cone of power are only limited by our imagination. The key is the rise of kundalini through the couple leading the rite. This is powerful. Frankly, we have wondered if the ritualist couples who lead the Great Rite with chalice and blade will make it all the way home for their own celebration. The power of this rite to arouse passion should not be underestimated.

Maithuna: Merging identities in sex

Maithuna is the Sanskrit word for union, creating one out of two. We can generate a model for creating one out of two, unity out of duality, with sacred sex. Even though some consider this to be purely a mental and symbolic act, its deep wisdom is found in physical sex. In the sexual union of body and spirit we merge into our sacred other and she or he into us. Our human selves and divine selves merge. Neither sex without meditation nor meditation without sex will reach that transcendence of self. One of us becomes the Goddess. The other becomes the God. Many of us understand they are literally present in our coupling.

However, if we free our kundalini we experience a form of *maithuna* without intercourse. In tantra, Shakti and Shiva share arousal through their emotional, mental and spiritual bodies without sexual penetration. That passion is shared with the human couple from the Gods. Our souls must be prepared for that union or it won't work. We need to know we have energy bodies or auras surrounding our physical form. We consciously release the chakras to work in those bodies, which we can think of as heart, mind and soul.

How do we do that? For a couple this merging begins with the physical contact of holding, kissing and caressing. The sexual arousal increases with thoughtful, loving physical contact in which partners open themselves to each other without reservation. The emotional body is engaged sexually when the feelings of love and acceptance along with the conscious touching and blending of the emotional aura and the chakras arouse deep feelings of adoration. Words of love and comfort assist partners in opening to this level of trust. The mental body is engaged as we remember to reach up and out of ourselves to include the Divine in our lovemaking. We may have invited them in prior to the first kiss, but a mental call to join our human bodies opens the mind to the ecstasy present in our physical and emotional union. When they arrive, our spiritual bodies resonate with another octave of experience. The barriers dissolve and we are indeed one.

Sadly, we do not all have human partners who are prepared for this experience. Some people are freaked out by the possibility of joining with the Gods in bed. Using a variation of the Circuit of Force meditation from Dion Fortune we developed the Web PATH Center's Safe Sex Meditation. This meditation works with the same and opposite sex identities we found earlier in our training. It is effective as a solitary meditation or as group meditation in which people connect with their Spirit Lovers. In some groups we have worked as human partners or with the group energy trading off on male and female roles. In those cases we may work without spouses or our usual partners, relying on our circle instead.

Safe Sex Meditation

Begin in meditation alone or with likeminded others in a sacred space. Breathe deeply all the way down into your belly and in time with others in the room. Enjoy long deep cleansing breaths and relax with your eyes closed. Mentally and emotionally reach out to your opposite sex self. Call that one to sit before you, as close and intimately as possible, consciously inside each other's emotional aura. Wrap your legs around each other in your imagination.

When the connection is made, women direct their breath to inhale from their vaginas up to the heart and then exhale out of the crown, then pause. Men breathe in from the crown down to their hearts and then exhale down from their hearts and out through the penis, then pause. During that pause, we envision our opposite sex partner receiving and drawing in the energy we released with our breath. We continue breathing this way for several breaths, knowing that the breaths are cycling through our opposite sex self so we share the same breath: in from his head, through his body out from his genitals in through her genitals, up to her heart, out through her crown and then in through his crown and down to continue the cycle. If we are seated in a room with other humans, each of us is experiencing this with our own opposite.

When the cycle is well established we reverse the direction of the breath so the women breathe in from the crown to heart and out from heart through vagina to their opposite sex self. Men inhale through penis to heart and out from heart to crown into their opposites' crowns. When that cycle is repeated numerous times we reverse again, maybe several times. We allow the breath and the rising energy to make the internal contact vividly sensual. We learn about our bodies, understand our feelings, discover thoughts and beliefs, and merge with other aspects of ourselves. As the merger grows, we unite with others in the room. Because our alternative selves are also aspects of the Divine, the Gods and Goddesses are present in this loving. We may or may not reach physical orgasm, but we are aroused. If the kundalini rises, an internal orgasm resonates through our bodies and extends to humans and spirits in the circle.

When our connection with each other and All Being is

complete, we begin our return to ordinary reality with our breath. We let the heightened energy fall down through us into the earth as we inhale through the nose and exhale through the mouth. We wrap our arms around ourselves in a hug. Then we stand and embrace others in the circle, giving thanks and honor as we return to our individual beings. Once everyone in the group returns to the sacred circle in everyday space and time we ground and release the excess energy into the earth, usually with our hands flat on the ground.

Ecstatic Energy

In discussing *maithuna* and merger, Missy reminded us that in any meditation the energy that flows through the body is ecstatic if we allow ourselves to feel it. Everyone has a ritually prompted experience with the Divine whether it be a spirit speaking through the inner ear or a God or Goddess entering the body. She knows first-hand actual sexual penetration or envelopment is not necessary for the bliss of orgasm to take over. Shortly after her Reiki 3 attunement the ecstasy spiraled through her, climbing and escalating, making every part of her physical being hum until the rush of orgasm hit her. She explained that through all this we learn to love 'all' of ourselves, every bit, every quirk. We learn we are as perfect as we are supposed to be at that moment as love flows through our bodies. Missy's energy flowed out to those around her. She shared the love with them as it streamed back and forth washing everyone in pleasure. She had not expected this before the Reiki attunement.

Our shared kundalini brings us together at the level of a deeper consciousness as we merge with each other and All Being. The rapport builds our community. We are more loyal and loving to each other when we hold this intimate connection around the circle. In the Western world people imagine that life is subdivided into two sides – sometimes opposing sides – such as light and dark, male and female, good and evil. This artificial dualism often works against women. A dualistic universe supports the illusion of congruence between dark, feminine and evil. No dualistic religious or philosophical system has been able to explain the divisions as something other than positive and negative (female gets the negative) in any way that is satisfactory. Dualism also works against community, forcing us apart. Consequently, our focus in the Web is on the greater unity reaching beyond light and dark, positive and negative as an adventure in spirituality. *Maithuna* is an alternative to dualism. *Maithuna* gathers the many and weaves them into one.

Not only does *maithuna* connect individuals into the community, it reunites our esoteric bodies into a single co-operative and shares that with our lover. When the body and the emotions open during intercourse, the mind or mental body begins to dissolve and connect in new ways with the other person. Telepathy increases. We know what will stimulate and please the partner before being told. Our rhythm and breath synchronize. We open our eyes and connect together as we create a new one out of the two of us. No one is dominant. No one is submissive. Logical thought becomes irrelevant. Thinking is replaced by knowing. This sexual path is a wisdom path, which grows out of being present together, not doing sex. Having an orgasm, making love, acting on each other's pleasure zones is surpassed by the merger of being. Oneness rises up from *maithuna*.

When the spirits merge, the bodies may not even move. The contact is total body, total heart, total mind and total spirit. We feel pulsing micro movements of the soul, moving from one to two, back and forth in harmony and then in unison, experiencing what it is like to be complete in both forms and in no form. We experience a cosmic explosion into tiny molecules throughout the universe. Then we know we are all things and nothing and this thing. This is *le petit mort*, the little death, which the French call orgasm, but it is beyond orgasm. *Maithuna* reflects the shamanic journey into death as it joins the cosmos in the most perfect joy of being and non-being that defies all explanation.

The experience of *maithuna* offers us a celebration of sexuality. When we transform the known into the unknown we find sacred sex. This is the Great Rite. It is also our right, but embracing sexual *maithuna* means we are forever transformed, changed and unlike who we were before.

Chapter 3

Recognizing the Chakras in Sex Magick

Readers may know about the main chakras when they begin sex magick, but here is a quick reference. When this information is new instruction, people need time to absorb the chakra material. It is quite foreign to our culture. Anodea Judith's video *The Illuminated Chakras* is a visual feast for chakra studies. We use it repeatedly to teach people about their emotional and spiritual bodies. The video shows the chakras working as gears, each connecting to the next chakra and turning in alternating directions as the kundalini snakes rises. Not everyone agrees. Some see them as all operating deosil. We work with people according to their own understanding of chakras so readers should adjust the instructions to suit their view.

How to Clear Chakras

First we ground and center. We begin with the root chakra at the base of the spine between our legs in the area of our sex organs. A hand held 4-6 inches away from the chakra can sense that energy center. Connecting with the chakra, we mentally check it for brightness of color, openness and size. It may be facing downward and attached to the tail bone or forward parallel to the pubis. Either is okay, but it should be straight in one direction or the other, not tilted. Our root chakra is bright ruby red, turning clockwise, and open. If not, we repair it through visualization. We see it as it should be, stirring it up with one hand and removing any debris or mud located there. We throw the debris into a green flame (also visualized) so it is consumed and transformed. This is a magickal act of healing. We act it out with no inhibitions.

The second chakra is below the naval and attached to the

spine. It should be facing forward, at right angles to the spine (this is true of all of the rest except the crown chakra). It is bright mandarin orange, turning counter clockwise and about half way or a third open in its center. Chakras open and close like a camera lens. We can open or close a chakra as we stir it up. Working in the same direction of the energy flow opens it. Working in reverse begins to close it. We never close them off entirely, but the belly chakra can pick up other people's feelings, symptoms or emotional illness, so it is good to monitor and clean this chakra closely.

The third chakra is at the solar plexus (stomach), attached to the spine. It should be bright yellow like the sun, turning clockwise and about half way open. This is a powerful center related to our Higher Self and our ability to manifest or create our desires.

The fourth chakra is at the heart attached to the spine. It should be bright pink or green like an emerald, turning counter clockwise and more than half way open, as long as one is comfortable with that. Our spiritual, emotional and psychic growth works toward a fully opened heart chakra. However, people with a closed and defended heart chakra rarely wish to move immediately to a receptive and open heart center. People find that vulnerability disorienting and perhaps frightening. We work on opening our heart chakras in reasonable increments.

The fifth chakra is at the throat and attached to the spine. It should be brilliant light blue like pure lake water under the sun, or a clear aquamarine crystal, turning clockwise and wide open. This is our center of communication. If our words are disregarded, if we cannot or choose not to speak our truth constructively, this chakra will be occluded. Gossip, lies, and hateful speech shut this chakra down. In clearing it we rely on a spirit of love from the heart. Connecting heart and throat begins a path of compassion and finding our voice.

The sixth chakra is at the third eye on the forehead between the eye brows and up slightly. It should be deep, clear indigo, turning counter clockwise and about half way open unless we are engaged in psychic or visionary work. We open it fully when we work magick or ritual. We reduce the opening when we finish. There is no need to be taking in psychic visions when washing dishes or parenting children.

The seventh chakra is at the crown of the head facing upward toward the sky. It should be purple or lavender (in our experience) and represents our connection to the Goddess. It turns clockwise and is wide open. We wish to remain connected to the Goddess at all times, so we leave it open.

The eighth chakra is above the crown of the head out about an arm's length. This is the transpersonal point, and should be clear white light, turning counter clockwise and is wide open. This is our point of merger with the universal All Being.

Once we have seen the chakras, assessed their clarity and added white light where it needs to be to increase their brightness and translucence, we go back and scan them to see if they are all the same size. They should be. We can move energy from one to another to balance them out. An over-active, over-large chakra will pull energy from its neighbors so they will be smaller or less energetic. Similarly a small, blocked chakra will back up energy in the neighboring chakras so they may be enlarged. We proceed with great gentleness in mending the chakras.

Chakra clearing is important in bringing the high energy of kundalini all the way through the body. If that power is stopped at a different chakra instead of piercing the crown, it dissipates. If it rises all the way through the body, it reaches out and links with All Being. However, the heart and crown chakras easily pick up relationship clutter from everyday life. We should clear them before ritual work with our circle of friends so the energy is free to flow as the ritual builds. On a personal level, if we practice clearing our own chakras on a daily basis, we can share this experience quite easily with our lover when we begin our lovemaking, whether we intend spell magick, healing or passion.

We need to create magick to bring us closer to clearness and clarity about ourselves and the beings we love. Our sexual passions help in that magick.

Engaging the Chakras in Sacred Sex

Ideally sacred sex connects all the chakras in all the bodies: physical, emotional, mental and spiritual. In practical terms, if we can run the sexual arousal through the physical chakras, we are doing well. The obvious question follows. How do we grab energy and move it through the chakras? Several meditative practices assist: visualization, breath, sound, and movement. Using those during intercourse is effective when both partners know what is happening. Otherwise, the experience can be disconcerting.

Visualization

When we can see our chakras in our mind's eye we can imagine the entwining strands of kundalini running through them. Visualize the energy coiled in the root chakra and then rising through the body to crisscross six times through the body chakras and joining in the transpersonal point helps open the pathway for the kundalini. These strands of energy are typically seen as great snakes, an image that is sacred in Asia and slightly horrifying in the West. Either we work through our snake phobia to welcome their wildness into our bodies, or we find another image. Perhaps seeing the DNA molecule as a pulsing white light energy will work as well. In either case, if we have practiced that double helix spiral of power working its way through our bodies often enough prior to using it in lovemaking, then the image will float automatically through us and around our kisses and caresses. The root chakra energy begins to uncoil with the first caresses as we anticipate our passionate encounter growing into intercourse. It winds upward through the belly chakra and stomach chakra. If we are also aware of our passionate love for the person we are and the person we make love with, then the energy rises into the heart. Resistance at the heart level reveals barriers in our love, which we may have been loath to admit. Forgiveness and compassion will open the heart chakra further. The kundalini does not allow us to lie to ourselves.

Having filled the heart chakra, the energy rises to the throat where it is encouraged by words of ecstasy. We sometimes hesitate to make noise, but night music helps the passion, compassion and kundalini flow. From the overflowing throat, we visualize the energy crossing at our brow and again at the crown. These chakras are spiritually enlightened locations that free up psychic skills and connection to the Gods. Piercing them with sexual energy requires courage. We are transformed by this level of ecstasy.

The energy spirals meet above our heads where the transpersonal point spins. The name itself describes what happens. The prefix *trans* means across or beyond. The word *personal* references our identity. This transpersonal point brings us up and out of ourselves to link across to our soul connection with All Being. When our very personal sexual energy rises through the body and connects with the Universe, we are transformed and empowered to be more.

We can visualize the snakes exchanging their energy at the transpersonal point. The energy of each then spirals down the other side of the double helix and returns to the root. From there it ascends again and repeats the rising and falling cycle of kundalini until it all explodes in a magnificent orgasm. When we have practiced and planned in advance, that orgasmic energy empowers the spell or magickal working we set up in the beginning.

Breath

Similarly, we can breathe into each chakra as we feel the energy rising. Breathing meditation (pranayama) is helpful for people who are not visual people. Again practice prior to intercourse helps the centers come alive with the focused breath despite the delightful distractions of sex. When the breath sticks in the throat and fails to infuse a chakra we find our energy blocks. The location is instructive. A blockage in the belly means there is something stuck that we should release either as a birth from our creative womb or as dross we should expel from our guts. Blockages in the solar plexus are situations we cannot stomach. Blockages in the heart show a failure or fear in love. Blockages in the throat show hindrances in speaking our truth. Blockages in the brow cover things we refuse to see or know. Blockages in the crown cut us off from divine awareness; in the transpersonal point we are separated from the Divine Being.

Sound

Musical people may wish to tone each other's chakras as an encouragement to the kundalini. The root chakra is 'C' and the others proceed up the musical scale. The syllables lam, vam, ram, yam, ham (with long ah vowels), Aum and Ah take us through the crown. The transpersonal point sits in silence or OM (Aum). Lying in an embrace, placing our hands over each other's chakras and toning together while locking our gaze is deeply sensual. The intimacy is so strong, we may dissolve in fits of giggles until we get used to it. The readiness is all.

Movement

We can engage in dance or yoga to open our chakras. To include that in our sexual passions, we may disrobe as we go along, or practice naked. Watching our partners perform or performing ourselves is a very sensual experience that pushes us past our barriers about beauty and body image. When we accept our bellies as rounded goblets of the Goddess and no long rue their shape and size, the sensual energy will flow through them. Two people dancing nude to slow sensual music, consciously opening their chests and torso instead of protecting them, rotating their hips in slow figure of eight patterns, stretching out their throats in total vulnerability, closing their eyes to see their lover and their Gods with the third eye, all the while psychically drawing the partner's energy closer and winding it about them frees the sexual energy to rise through the body.

When the sexual energy is free in our bodies, our lovemaking directs itself. We remember as we love that the ecstasy is for ourselves, our Gods and our magick. At the orgasmic release, the energy is sent to the altar, to our hearts or to the Universe depending on our purposes for sacred sex.

Chapter 4

Spirit Lovers

Who Are They?

Spirit Lovers join us in a loving and sexual relationship in a variety of personas. How we understand their identity depends on who we think the Gods, Goddesses, elementals, ancestors, guides and shamanic allies are. These relationships may be explicit and physical, but they are also spiritual. Spirit Lovers themselves are unfettered by a distinctive physical form. Their appearance may be consistent as angels or deceased friends. It may vary when they are elementals or plant and animal devas from the natural world.

Elly met the Forest God on Midsummer Night during a Web SummerFest. She was ready to exclude all men from her life, including the Patron consort to her Goddess. After a problematic marriage, a dishonest high priest in her first circle, an abusive employer, and her adored father who suddenly accused her of wasting his time with her problems, she was done with patriarchy. She came to SummerFest as a guest, disconnected from any tribe and hoping to be alone. The Goddess did not accept a lopsided spirituality, not at the Web.

After opening ritual, she withdrew to her new one-person tent with a good book, determined to block out the world for the weekend including all those friendly Webfolk. She was irritated by the drum circle, annoyed by the sounds of wildlife, and too angry to sleep. Lying on her sleeping bag she considered leaving for the night and coming back the next day. Suddenly firefly flashes morphed into a green flashlight beam headed at her. Grousing about people who can't find the privy in the dark, she held her breath as the campground went silent and someone worked the tent zipper open.

'Wrong tent, buddy,' she rasped, reliving all the crazed maniac stories she had ever heard. She fumbled for a light. The tent door flew open in the breeze. She waited, terrified, backed against the tent wall. No one was there. She smelled the soft green fragrance of deep forests pushed into the tiny space. The tent breathed with the wind. Outside sounds returned, water bubbling against rocks, a heartbeat of drumming, an owl hoot.

Elly stretched out in the wind that felt like a caress. It enveloped her, swirled around, rocked her and kissed her as if she were the most beloved of all. Enchanted, her anger and tension poured out on to the ground. She was afloat with beauty and lightness.

Then the heat built, first in her root and then up exquisitely slow through her body like gentle fingers massaging her womb, hips, belly like the sun, like hearth fire on a cold day, rising steadily. It took her lungs with a whoosh. She inhaled a rebirth into her heart, faster and faster. Choked with emotion she couldn't name she exploded with the light and went still. She was well loved, and finally knew it. In the morning, there were deer tracks at the front of her tent. Later a huge buck guarded her from a hill on her daily commute to work. She saw him standing tall against the sky, huge horns catching the light. Then he appeared in the woods at home. Once he ran alongside the car down the middle of the road for a mile or more, hooves clattering. Years later, when the healing was done, she saw him rise up from the sleeping form of her new beloved man, stare at her knowingly and vanish into the moonlight.

Satira relates a number of intriguing trysts including one on the Outer Banks of North Carolina. Some Webfolk attended *Teach at the Beach,* which is a thrill for land lubbers stuck hundreds of miles inland. Satira was so happy, she rushed to greet the ocean. Initially, the water was calm, with only small waves. As she waded into the surf, the water surrounded her gently and lovingly. As she danced about in the small waves, a sudden large surge of water rose up and pulled her top down around her waist! She squealed and laughed, pulling it back up, and we all joked that the ocean was getting 'frisky.' Then when Galadriel's back was turned, the sea slapped her on the bottom with a mysterious wave from nowhere. After that, we walked on the shore in the moonlight to find small gifts in polished, glistening bits of shell and the sight of ghost crabs inching along the sand. Once we found the tracks of newly hatched baby turtles. The ocean was seducing us to gather there, making romantic gestures toward us.

On one particular evening, Satira lay on the shore, allowing the ocean to wash over her body. The motion of the waves, the smell of the water, the salty taste of the ocean, were sensually akin to making love. Something extraordinary had happened, but we didn't understand it yet. Then we then had a shamanic journey session taught by Bekki Shining Bearheart and Crow to contact our Spirit Lovers. Satira had already met her lover, the ocean. She was then given a vision that left our entire group in awe. She was back with the ocean, lying on the beach being caressed with the waves. This tryst became a romantic sexual encounter within the context of the shamanic journey. In trance she conceived a spirit water child. The journey then took her to the dry heat of the desert where she trudged across the sand, extremely pregnant and suffering. Isis appeared full of concern and bundled her to an oasis with beautiful white tents. When Horus arrived, Satira birthed the water child. The baby became a spring in the desert. Satira and the Ocean created a well for the desert people who witnessed the birth. Together they celebrated its creation. Satira reports she has returned several times to visit the child who is growing, recognizing her relationship with the Ocean as father and Satira as mother. The girl child/spring is devoted to Isis who is very alive and acknowledged by those who live there.

This is not the first elemental lover Satira met. The wind in Montana near the Crow Agency blew through her and taught her history. It also fanned her inner fire then as it has at her home in New York, at our 2013 SummerFest and created ecstasy. Galadriel agreed that the wind's voice is present in these places as it talks to the trees. Satira reported dancing with a fire shaman in trance on that hill. They turned and twirled through the fire into crystalline structures with dragons spewing out double helix fires that looked like DNA. The fire spirits licked her body and aroused her fires to orgasm. In the western mountains she learned an erotic grounding. Most of these elemental spirits did not have a gender connection with the exception of the Ocean when she conceived.

Both Galadriel and Satira agree these contacts were mergers with the elements, not simple links, but deep mergers. Satira, who is a skilled channeler, said that spirit sex is the same as channeling. We receive messages all the time, all of us, and likely have intimate encounters with the spirits but turn away and pretend we don't. Channeling and sensual merger is for everyone.

People look at sacred sex with Spirit Lovers as mysticism when it is a natural experience. We need to understand their capabilities and learn to work with this vast energy of spiritual intimacy. If we take the mysticism out and expect our union with All That Is to complete our lives, then we can do anything. This union is how all of creation works. We have to unlearn our limitations. We are taught we cannot walk on water or create wealth from air. We fear breaking out into the impossible. We learn not to risk ourselves with Spirit Lovers or with miracles. All of that fear holds us back from full identity as magical loving beings.

On the other hand, Satira points out some human and spirit beings try to keep people ignorant on purpose. People can be kept down a long time, but not forever. Spiritual ecstasy is natural. Dionysus and Zeus chasing Goddesses and anything else that took their fancy speaks to the dynamic connections possible. The moralists imposed their fears and judgments on the stories. We learned many of them as rape fantasies, violent attacks, and heartbreaking betrayals. Satira asks if we really think Hera was so insecure when she is a Goddess of cities with a crown of stars? No. Our myths are skewed based on people's idea of what the moral of the story should be. They were meant to teach us love and merger with the Divine. Instead, the God's behavior is told in violent and frightening ways. Incubus and succubus contacts in the Christian era were condemned by the Church as demonic. Pagans have absorbed fear of possession and loss of control from our culture. But what is that orgasm in the middle of the night's sleep? That's fun. That's what it is! There is no harm in it.

So who was there when we wake up in a full body orgasm? Obviously someone. Galadriel encounters an angelic being in dreams and occasionally in ordinary reality standing in her kitchen. He is gorgeous, male, golden and erotic as well as spiritual. He says his name is David. He teaches and loves her. Anemone is visited by a dead lover from the Summerland as she sleeps. Others are wooed by spirits from past lives who keep a bond with their soulmates.

Spirit Lovers do things to get us to rethink our beliefs. Brigit kissed Satira at Imbolc erotically. The candle burst into the three flames to reassure Satira it was indeed Brigit. She was uncomfortable at first, but then reassured because the kiss was love and teaching together. Learning by butting up against a central belief (ritual etiquette does not include same sex romance) very quickly changes beliefs.

Spirit Lovers may also be historic figures. Satira reported meeting a known religious leader in spirit for teaching. Their long talks grew into a sensual relationship. Because he was a devoted religious man not open to affairs when he was alive, she felt uncomfortable and imposed constraints on it. Those were her limits not his. Others in the Web have met historic figures from their families, from their neighborhoods, from the headlines of long ago who come to them for love and healing. We can function as the sacred priestess, bridging the gap across the centuries to resolve a spirit's regrets or abuse as well as our own. Sometimes we discover these spirits are also lovers in this life working to resolve old issues. Sometimes there is a threesome or a foursome when you count the spirits in our beds.

The vast implications of Spirit Lovers among elementals, Gods, Goddesses and humans who have crossed over are mind boggling. We can't assimilate all those connections, and aren't meant to. When we leave earth we merge with All That Is which extends further and deeper than sexual merger. Certainly these experiences that prepare us for our ultimate merger exist outside the view of the moralist or priest. Unlearning their cultural lessons is mind boggling. Satira says the simplest way is to look at sacred spiritual sex as connection with pure energy and not figure things out. The thought process is difficult. On the other hand, some of us need to pick away at our biases and understand what it means when ethereal hands reach across the Void and hold us.

What Does a Spirit Lover Expect?

The vastness of a spirit merger in itself is sensual. Physics is erotic to Galadriel. The potential magick of spiritual merger makes her mind spark, which is the essence of sexuality. She sucks up expanded consciousness and it explodes in her whole body. But how does one get there? And once we have reached the Other on that level, what do they want? Is it safe?

Satira advises us to be in the right place for learning. Geography, relationships, education, spiritual practice need to support the possibilities. Then we must know we don't know. Seeing a practice from a different angle makes it all new, as with her kiss from Brigit. When we are stuck in facts, we shut down our potential. We need to be comfortable living with the truth that nothing is ever what we think. We spiral upward through various octaves of meanings so what we know about the elementals when we learn to cast a circle is only the beginning of what we know about them when we engage them face to face or sensually. Galadriel adds from her guide and lover, the angelic David, that we are being upgraded now, all around the world so our minds will link as bodies do. Our Spirit Lovers want this linkage.

Fears about what might be asked of us miss the point that Spirit Lovers love unconditionally. They are not judging us or our appearances. Petty things human lovers would pick at are not an issue. They have waited all our lives for this connection, and are willing to wait more. The relationships we have in spirit challenge our understanding of love. We need to listen to what they say without imposing our human experiences on their message. A particular spirit may have more than one human lover. A human may have more than one Spirit Lover. Promiscuity as a moral concept does not fit in the human-spirit alliance.

Keeping our Balance with Spirit Lovers

Balance in a relationship with entities who are disembodied and magickal can be difficult. It isn't something one discusses with a therapist because, in ordinary reality, it skirts the edge of madness. However, contact from the spirit world may be exactly what is misdiagnosed as mental illness. Rejection of spirit contact and subsequent breaks from reality may be an insistent spirit instead of hallucinations and delusions. So how can we proceed sanely?

First, the use of hallucinogens and/or substance abuse clouds everything and is harmful unless it is handled appropriately with someone who knows. That needs to be an ethical shaman, a trained ethnobotanist and teacher who is experienced with mushrooms or herbs. Truly, the Spirit Lover is available to an ordinary person without getting high. They may be less available when we are under the influence since the plant or chemical energy seeks to replace theirs.

Secondly, proceed with the caveat 'An you harm none,' which always includes the self. We are not giving over our power and authority to a spiritual entity. We are sharing each other's essence. If we have not worked out our boundaries and mergers in human sex, we will find the same issues as a point of challenge and learning with spirits. We do well to avoid imposing our ordinary reality beliefs on an extraordinary encounter. We also do well not to take the same openness and boundlessness of the sexual spiritual encounter and apply it to our human relations. Some things can be brought across, but much of it cannot. Intentional sex with one's human partner as discussed above will help keep our balance. Our human sense of unworthiness – I can't do that, I am not ideal – draws people back from humans and spirits. We intend to go beyond self-censorship and soar.

Third, credit what your experience is. We all wonder if spirit sex is a product of a wild imagination or a flight of fantasy. Accept the vision and physical response as real. It is not shameful. Enjoy the ride. Be as honest as you can with both yourself and the Spirit Lover, and let it evolve naturally. Relax and accept it is a natural experience. They are approaching us because they love us. Take a deep breath, be challenged and learn. The more we understand love and sex are the way of creation, the better off we are. They are here to give us to unconditional love expressed without limit or fear. We are taught what we can't be by our culture. The Gods and Goddesses try to teach us what is open and real.

Fourth, don't be homophobic about Spirit Lovers. You don't need a penis and vagina to engage in sacred sex. Any combination is acceptable. Our experience with Spirit Lovers may be explicitly physical or energetic without human physicality. Kissing Brigit in ritual was clearly physical. When Satira started to pull back, Brigit objected. Her feelings were hurt. At various times several of us have felt wings wrap around our bodies in ordinary reality. The enfolding embrace transcends into a merger of all bodies. Bekki who practices shamanism has sacred sex with selkie and bear as well as with Herne as a tree. She can feel is bark as skin and she makes love with a tree, only afterward wondering how is that possible?

The best explanation we have is based in our chakras. Most of our physical body sex centers in the root and sacral chakras. Clearing the channels with tantra, kundalini practices, yoga or the Circuit of Force brings all of the energy centers into the sexual experience. Sex with other-dimensional beings or non-human entities creates merger between chakras in two spirits, ours and theirs. Astral sex is similar to this.

So how does this aspect of sacred sex involve magick? It IS magick. People go through elaborate spells with crystals, candles and herbs to convince the human mind that magick will work. The spirits don't need that. The humans do. We can do magick without a big deal if we believe it. The power of sexuality and orgasm, auto, self, divine partner, plant or animal in shamanic experiences all work magick with the Spirit Lover who is any of those manifestations and more.

Chapter 5

Our Best Advice

When we engage in sacred sex magick, we are treading on exciting ground. We can be overcome. We take chances and extend our souls beyond our comfort zone. We can grow beyond any idea we ever had about who we are. We can also get in trouble. One woman we knew long before the Web was founded told about invoking a particular dynamic God as a Spirit Lover. She was new at magick and reached beyond her training. She had a rollicking good time, but then he wouldn't leave. Finally she had to admit to her teacher she was being stalked by Chango. Her teacher went up one side of her and down the other, so to speak. What was she thinking? She neither knew enough about him nor about the invocation process to experiment on her own. To avoid that sort of unpleasantness, our group compiled our best advice.

First, be impeccable about ethics. Ethics is defined as a moral code, which for pagans is a liminal territory. We have no big 10 thou-shalt-nots. What we have are the following guidelines.

An That You Harm None, Do What You Will
Harm is a relative term. We take it to mean deep soul-searing damage not hurt feelings. Hurt feelings are avoidable with love and consideration, but they do not rise to the level of harm. Betrayal, lies, broken promises, carelessness about safe sex and discounting our own partner's feelings create deep pain beyond hurt feelings. We avoid that.

However, soul pain works both ways. Hurting other people without consideration of their fears harms the doer's soul. Consequently, sex magick involving people without their consent or knowledge crosses the ethical line. Sacred sex practiced with someone else's partner without the absent other's knowledge or consent crosses the ethical line. We need to talk about these opportunities in tantric practice and agree on them. We need to speak ethically and honestly, not sneak around. When our spouse or committed partner says no or wait, we need to listen.

Love is the Whole of the Law, Love Under Will

Love is an essential part of the magick. It may not be the 'I want to marry you' love. It may not be romantic love. In fact, possessive marital and romantic love might work against the magick. Couples in throes of a new relationship may raise great energy with the lovemaking, but they may find it difficult to direct it outside of the bedroom (or living room, or hot tub, or where ever they are). The passion is personal and overwhelming in romantic love, understandably so. Sex in a romantic relationship is sacred just because it is wonderful. It fills up the empty spots and makes life beautiful. If a couple can take that excitement and passion and turn it to magickal workings, then so much the better. If they are so caught up in each other they forget there was another intention, then we say 'enjoy.' They can get back to this intentional magick stuff later.

On the other hand, sex without a deep regard and respect for the partner lacks the loving luster necessary for effective sex magick. There isn't enough sacredness about recreational sex with what's-his-name to create a decent cone of power.

This is where sex and love and magick can get tricky. Both parties must be mature enough to get lost in the experience, create deep pleasure in each other, and keep their heads about them to direct the orgasms into the magickal intent. Sacred sex cannot be mechanical and technically adept without deep caring about the other. Nor can sacred sex be effective with mushy, giggly, silly, romantic, are-we-the-only-ones-in-the-universe lovers who lose their focus.

The love present in sacred sex and effective sex magick is a dependable, passionate, and open love for the Gods and for ourselves. Both of ourselves. We want to love the Gods. We want to love our partners. If we do not love ourselves with all our heart, then we will fall short with the others.

Anemone points out the kind of love that works best in sacred sex and magick is an openhanded, unpossessive love that recognizes we are both here because we want to be here, for ourselves, for the other one, and for the Gods. It is a threesome with the spirits involved. As we do not have ownership of the deities who join in our passion, neither do we have ownership of our partner. We do own our bodies, heart and soul. We willingly and enthusiastically join them with a human partner and/or a spirit partner. We are all involved in the adoration of each other. To think that the Gods adore us can be challenging on very basic levels. This idea is not the common knowledge of our times. Yet it is true.

The Rule of Three: What We Send Out is Returned Threefold.

This is a philosophical adage, not a math formula. We reap what we sow, in this life or maybe later. Instant karma is rare. Nevertheless, what goes around comes around eventually. If the imperative of love and doing no harm is insufficient to keep us from manipulating naïve people who haven't the strength of personality to say NO to a sexual situation with a powerful priest or priestess, then our understanding of payback might help. Older mentors have a great deal of authority over younger students. Teachers should be careful about forming romantic or sexual relationships with students. Sacred sex is a partnership of peers.

Everyone Should Use Safe Sex Practices

Condoms are required outside of committed relationships. There are too many sexually transmitted diseases around to be careless, even once. Someone asked if birth control disrupts the magickal energy flow. The answer is, not so much as unplanned pregnancies and +HIV status will. We have logical minds, scientific training joined with unconditional love and magickal skill for many reasons. One of them is so we can be smart about our spirituality. It is not smart (read stupid) to think that because a sexual encounter is joined with the Gods and is sacred, then we can't get pregnant or contract a disease. We are also humans. Humans get pregnant. Humans get sexually transmitted diseases. The Gods do not overrule that.

What about birth control? What about failure in birth control?

The heterosexual couple engaging in sacred sex and magick should talk about these things. Assuming the partner has adequate birth control and would not want another child without a deep discussion is silly, and yet people do that. If we don't know each other well enough to discuss birth control, we don't know each other well enough to engage in sacred sex.

In observing these ethical guidelines, we practice balance and equality between the partners. Underage people are not able to participate in a literal Great Rite ceremony though the symbolic Great Rite seems appropriate for them. We do not use intercourse in our initiation. People need to know if intercourse is an expectation before joining a group. There should be considerable communication to work through the implications. Underage initiations in those circumstances are legally prohibited.

Web initiations are intended as acts of empowerment from the group to the initiate. People who have less sexual and magickal experience as an apprentice cannot hold their own power in equal portions to the adepts in our circle. We leave it to the Gods and Goddesses to bring them along in increments that make sense for their own history. Spiritual growth is a complex process. An initiation opens the door to later insights. Sex magick fits in once the relationships between human and spirits are clearer for the individual. Even with Spirit Lovers we seek equity and balance.

Encouraging Sensuality in Pagan Society

Some people find discomfort in sensuality. They suspect motives. They recoil from contact with people other than their spouse or children. They are unready for sexual magick. Those individuals need to wait until the time is right. On the other hand, for people ready to increase their sensitivity and connect with the world through the sense of touch and the experience of live, there are some practices that can help. Foot washing, pentacle meditations, and Margo Anand's Inner Flute meditation all open up our sensuality.

Foot Washing

As part of our Wicca III instruction our body work 'kicks off' with the feet. We challenge ourselves to love our feet and make no judgments about them. Never mind if we trimmed our toenails recently, have cracks and calluses, or dry skin. These feet do a wonderful job for us in getting us where we are going! They are loved and pampered by pagan foot washing.

Working with someone other than our usual partner, the first washer gets towels, a foot tub with comfortably warm water in it, scented soap and body lotion or massage oil while the other sits and relaxes. When we are set up, we gaze into each other's eyes, getting in touch with the inner child of other person. People giggle and release the tension because the experience is outside of the norm. We pay attention to our own physical sensations as one person takes one of the other's feet and puts it in the water. The first foot washer touches the foot in the bath according to what feels good to the toucher, being selfish about that. We touch with fingers, palms, and the back of the hand across all the foot surfaces as we wash our partner's feet. We are light hearted not reaching for therapeutic massage. This is for pleasure and fun. When both feet are stroked and washed, the washer gets fresh water to rinse the feet. We rinse the feet carefully and dry them. Then we use lotion or oils on the skin, making sure it is a pleasurable scent to both people.

The receiver allows free access to the feet and practices being comfortable accepting touch, nurturing, love. If there is pain, we give immediate feedback. Otherwise, we sit back and let it happen. Be aware of memories, fears, or fantasies that surface. When time is up, both people may wish to make some notes. Some people find this exercise more difficult than others. If it seems too easy, we go deeper into the experience of letting go so our feet are completely held and controlled by another. We resist all impulses to move our feet, to lift them in or out of the water. That is for your partner to do.

If it is difficult for you, tell your partner. Let him or her help you work through your resistance to being touched. Make some notes and insights on foot washing.

Then switch places.

Iron Pentacle Meditation

The Reclaiming Tradition of Wicca taught by Starhawk includes several pentacle meditations. The Iron Pentacle joins sex, identity, passion, pride and power through a virtual pentacle laid over the body. Anemone indicates this clears conflicted energy and empowers the individual to experience the whole body physically and emotionally.

Begin lying on the floor with arms stretched out to the side and legs apart so the body looks like a five-pointed star. Center and ground. Focus attention on the points of the star. Be aware of each one in turn, and assign them the following meanings. Say the word out loud and let it sink into that body part. Let images and replies from the body surface into consciousness. Remember what the body has to say. First work around the body deosil so each point has its correspondent.

Begin with the head. Focus attention to the head, brain and glands. This is the top point of the star. It represents sex. Let your head talk to you about sex.

When you are ready, focus attention on your left hand stretched out to the side. This point represents Self, your identity, the totality of you. Let your left hand talk to you about who you are. Don't argue. Just take it in and understand. Ask questions and hear yourself.

Next, focus attention on your left foot. Feel what it is like reaching out into one of the lower points of the star. This is what the star stands on. The left foot represents passion. Let your foot talk to you about desire, intensity, and all that you love. Feel how passion grows in you, and how it enters your foot.

Focus your attention on your right foot. Sense it reaching into the other base of the star. The right foot represents pride. Let your foot talk to you about your accomplishments, your skills, your pleasure with yourself (found in your left hand). Encourage the dialog and list of things to celebrate about yourself. Toot your own horn. You are supposed to.

Focus on your right hand. This point represents your power, your sense of control, personal magick, and ability to make things happen. Point your index finger and feel the power build up behind it. Listen to your hand talk about what it has done and wishes to do. This point has the power to manifest the desires of your heart. See how it is connected to the heart as well as the other points.

Now return to the head and circle around the five points naming the correspondence until they are clear in your mind. Sex, self, passion, pride and power. Let them swill around you. Then draw the invoking pentacle over your body saying the points in that order: head/sex; right foot/pride; left hand/self; right hand/power; left foot/passion; and back to head/sex. Repeat many times until you have woven a pentacle with no beginning or ending. Be still in the midst of the swirling energy, letting it move through you until it slows of its own accord. Then circle widdershins around your body with the fading energy to release the vortex you have created. Head/sex, right hand/power, right foot/pride, left foot passion, left hand self/and return to head/sex. Circle slowly three times or more if you need to. Let the pentacle rest easily on your body and disburse it with your breath. Sit up. Ground and center. Make any notes you wish.

Inner Flute Meditation

Margo Anand in *The Art of Sexual Ecstasy* teaches the opening of the inner flute. This is the kundalini channel beginning at the perineum and moving up through the center of the body to the crown chakra. Basically the Inner Flute meditation takes sexual and sensual arousal and moves it up the body instead of out of the body. This practice transfers a genital orgasm to full body ecstasy. Anand points out that the Inner Flute connects the major glands of the body, which correspond to the chakras:

- Testes or ovaries (root and belly chakra)
- Pancreas (solar plexus)
- Adrenals (solar plexus)
- Thymus (heart)
- Thyroid (throat)
- Pituitary (brow)
- Pineal (brow and crown)
- Hypothalamus (crown)

To play the Inner Flute as a breath meditation, set up a half-hour meditation in sacred space. Work naked or in comfortable loose clothing so your sensations are able to move freely within you. Breathe through the open mouth, in and out. Anand suggests pursing your mouth as a nursing child or as in oral sex. See if that makes a difference.

When you have the breath working easily through your body, up and down the chakra system, add a gentle squeeze from your PC muscles, the ones you use to control urination or to push with during childbirth. Inhale and contract the PC muscles. Exhale and relax them. Inhale through your genitals carrying the breath up to the crown. Exhale down your body and back out your genitals.

Visualize the path of the breath through the glands and organs, through the chakras so it becomes literal and real. They will vibrate with the breath, though your awareness of them may be gradually increased over time. So much of our body sleeps. This breath meditation is an internal awakening. Let it happen at its own pace. The pathway you are clearing and awakening is the same pathways kundalini follows. This breathing practice will create an awareness of kundalini energy in your body. It is already there.

Spell to be Free of an Old Lover

Begin by taking a ritual bath or shower. As you soap up and rinse off, say, 'All the places he (she) touched are new this day.' When you are finished, imagine you are bathed in white light, brilliant as the sun. Say, 'I am brand new, starting over. I belong to myself and no one else.'

Then place two chairs facing each other about six feet apart. You will sit in one. Imagine your old flame is seated in the other. Breathe deeply and ground. Brighten the white light around you and realize s/he has no hold over you anymore. This is a new day and a new way to be. If you need to rant and rage you can do this. Otherwise, save your breath and say simply, 'It is over between us. I release you completely. I take back my power. You have no claim on me.' Say it as many times as needed so you and your ex believe this.

Then narrow your eyes so you can see the energy flowing between you. They are like strands of light, various colors and clarity. At each end of the stand is a hook. One end is hooked into your ex at the heart, gut, genitals or elsewhere. One end is hooked into you. Unhook yourself as many times as there are strands of light between you. Say, 'I am not hooked on you anymore. I am free,' every time you remove a hook.

Tell your virtual ex to remove the same hooks as you remove yours so your ex is freed from you. If the imaginary lover will not do this, then reach out and unhook the other end of the strand yourself. You can kind of flip it out without hurting or touching your ex.

When all the hooks are gone, imagine gathering the light strands up into a ball on the floor. Then imagine them '*Poof!*' disappearing.

Tell your imaginary ex to leave you alone, except for any conversation you need to have about children or property. Say you are not open to him or her, cannot be manipulated or controlled. Then say goodbye firmly without regret and watch your ex leave.

Put the chairs back where they belong. Dust them or wash them.

If you have any trinkets left over from your days together, gather them up and get rid of them once and for all. Then give thanks to your Goddess. Do something else nice for yourself.

Summary

Enjoying the ecstasy of sex magick while remaining grounded and ethical is a responsible commitment. We observe the laws of our land and bar minors from inappropriate experiences. We tell the truth. We keep our promises. We recognize the rule of three and the power of love. If we feel blocked from sensuality and wish to open ourselves, we encourage our bodies to experience pleasure and love. We heal the wounds carried from old relationships. We welcome the pleasure of the Gods. We raise sexual power through ordinary pagan practices like grounding, building energy and casting spells. We dare love deeply and profoundly. Ultimately, we become one with the Divine, if only during the trembling of orgasm. An empowered sensual pagan can do wonders. We create magic with our bodies, minds and spirits only to learn it is all a woven piece of spiritual cloth, a tapestry of our individual truth and a blanket of protection. The best part about sex magick is that it takes a good deal of practice.

MOON
BOOKS

Moon Books invites you to begin or deepen your encounter with
Paganism, in all its rich, creative, flourishing forms.